WebGL Wizardry: A Beginner's Guide to Interactive 3D Graphics

WebGL Wizadry

Kameron Hussain and Frahaan Hussain

Published by Kameron Hussain, 2024.

WEBGL WIZARDRY: A BEGINNER'S GUIDE TO INTERACTIVE 3D GRAPHICS

First edition. January 18, 2024.

ISBN: 979-8224273386

Written by Kameron Hussain and Frahaan Hussain.

Table of Contents

Social Media:

Online Communities:

16.4. Networking and Community Involvement

Attend Conferences and Meetups:

Join Online Groups:

Collaborate:

16.5. Finding Opportunities in WebGL Development

Job Search:

Freelancing:

Start Your Own Projects:

Education and Training:

Chapter 16: Building a WebGL Portfolio

16.1. Planning Your Portfolio Projects

Define Your Goals:

Showcase a Range:

Quality Over Quantity:

Tell a Story:

Include Personal Projects:

16.2. Effective Presentation of 3D Work

Clear Project Titles and Descriptions:

High-Quality Visuals:

Interactive Demos:

Code Samples and Technical Details:

User Experience (UX):

Testimonials and Recommendations:

Continuous Updates:

Accessibility:

16.3. Building an Online Presence

1. Portfolio Website:

2. Social Media:

3. Blogging and Content Creation:

4. Online Communities and Forums:

5. GitHub and Open Source Contributions:

6. Online Courses and Webinars:

7. Attend Virtual Conferences and Webinars:

8. Personal Branding:

9. Networking:

10. Online Security and Privacy:

16.4. Networking and Community Involvement

1. Join WebGL Communities:

2. Participate in Discussions:

3. Attend WebGL Meetups and Conferences:

4. Collaborate on Projects:

5. Contribute to Open Source:

6. Create Educational Content:

7. Attend Web Development and Game Development Events:

8. Engage on Social Media:

9. Offer Workshops or Webinars:

10. Be Respectful and Professional:

11. Stay Informed:

16.5. Finding Opportunities in WebGL Development

1. Game Development Studios:

2. Web Development Agencies:

3. E-learning and EdTech:

4. Augmented and Virtual Reality:

5. Creative Agencies:

6. Freelancing:

7. Start Your Own Projects:

8. Education and Training:

9. Research and Development:

4. Machine Learning and AI

5. Web 3.0 and Decentralized Graphics

6. Accessibility and Inclusivity

7. Environmental Considerations

8. Collaboration and Standards

9. Education and Training

10. Ethical and Privacy Considerations

Chapter 1: Introduction to WebGL

1.1. Understanding WebGL and Its Capabilities

WebGL, short for Web Graphics Library, is a JavaScript API for rendering interactive 3D and 2D graphics within web browsers. It brings the power of hardware-accelerated graphics to web applications, enabling developers to create immersive and visually stunning web experiences. In this section, we'll dive into the fundamentals of WebGL and explore its capabilities.

What is WebGL?

WebGL is a web-based standard developed by the Khronos Group that allows developers to access the GPU (Graphics Processing Unit) on a user's computer directly from the web browser. It's built on top of the OpenGL ES (Embedded Systems) standard, which is a widely-used graphics API. WebGL enables high-performance rendering of 3D graphics, making it possible to create games, simulations, data visualizations, and interactive 3D applications directly in the browser.

Key Features of WebGL

WebGL offers several key features that make it a powerful tool for web developers:

1. **Hardware Acceleration:** WebGL leverages the GPU's parallel processing capabilities, allowing for complex graphics computations to be offloaded from the CPU. This results in smoother and more responsive graphics rendering.

2. **Cross-Platform Compatibility:** WebGL is supported by major web browsers, including Chrome, Firefox, Safari, and Edge, making it a cross-platform solution for delivering 3D content to users.
3. **Integration with HTML and JavaScript:** WebGL seamlessly integrates with HTML and JavaScript, enabling developers to create interactive web applications that combine 3D graphics with standard web content.
4. **Real-Time Rendering:** With WebGL, you can achieve real-time rendering of 3D scenes, making it suitable for applications that require dynamic updates, such as games and simulations.

How WebGL Works

WebGL works by providing a JavaScript API that allows developers to interact with the GPU. Here's a simplified overview of the process:

1. **Setting Up the Canvas:** Developers create an HTML5 canvas element in their web page, which serves as the drawing surface for WebGL.
2. **Context Creation:** In JavaScript, a WebGL context is obtained by calling canvas.getContext('webgl') or canvas.getContext('webgl2') depending on the version of WebGL you want to use.
3. **Shader Programs:** WebGL relies on shaders, which are small programs executed on the GPU. Developers write vertex and fragment shaders to define how objects are rendered.
4. **Data and Buffers:** Data such as vertices, textures, and colors are uploaded to the GPU using buffers. These buffers contain the information needed to render objects.
5. **Rendering Pipeline:** The rendering process involves vertex

processing, fragment processing, and rasterization. Shaders play a crucial role in determining how objects are transformed and colored.

6. **Drawing Commands:** Developers issue drawing commands to render objects using the WebGL context. These commands specify which shader program to use, which buffers to bind, and how to render the objects.
7. **Interactivity:** WebGL applications can respond to user input, making it possible to create interactive 3D experiences. This often involves handling mouse and keyboard events.

Browser Support and Compatibility

WebGL is widely supported in modern web browsers, but it's essential to check compatibility for specific features and performance considerations. WebGL2, introduced as an extension to WebGL, provides additional features and improved performance, but it may not be available in all browsers.

In the next sections of this chapter, we will explore the evolution of 3D graphics on the web, compare WebGL with other graphics technologies, and guide you through setting up your development environment for WebGL projects.

Stay tuned as we take our first steps into the exciting world of WebGL and start creating a basic WebGL template.

1.2. The Evolution of 3D Graphics on the Web

The evolution of 3D graphics on the web has been a remarkable journey, transforming the way we interact with online content and applications. In this section, we'll explore the key milestones and advancements that have paved the way for WebGL and 3D web graphics.

Early Web Graphics

In the early days of the web, graphics were primarily limited to 2D images, animated GIFs, and basic HTML layouts. The web was mainly a text-based medium, and interactive multimedia content was limited by the capabilities of browsers and internet connections.

Introduction of Plugins

As the demand for richer web experiences grew, plugins like Adobe Flash and Java applets emerged. These plugins allowed developers to create interactive animations and games that went beyond the capabilities of standard HTML and CSS. However, they came with their own set of limitations, including compatibility issues and security concerns.

The Rise of WebGL's Predecessors

WebGL's development was influenced by previous attempts to bring 3D graphics to the web. Technologies like VRML (Virtual Reality Modeling Language) and X3D (Extensible 3D) aimed to enable 3D content in web browsers but faced limited adoption due to complex authoring and plugin dependencies.

Introduction of Canvas and SVG

HTML5 brought significant changes to web development by introducing the <canvas> element and Scalable Vector Graphics (SVG). The <canvas> element allowed for dynamic 2D graphics rendering using JavaScript, while SVG provided a vector-based approach for creating scalable and interactive graphics. These technologies marked a shift towards more dynamic and visually appealing web content.

Emergence of WebGL

WebGL emerged as a standard in 2011, backed by major browser vendors and the Khronos Group. It was designed to bring hardware-accelerated 3D graphics directly to web browsers without the need for plugins. WebGL builds on the OpenGL ES standard and provides a low-level API that allows developers to access the GPU's power for rendering 3D scenes.

WebGL's Impact

WebGL's adoption has been significant, revolutionizing the web by enabling the development of 3D games, interactive simulations, data visualizations, and immersive VR experiences—all within the browser. Its portability across different platforms and browsers has made it a versatile tool for both entertainment and practical applications.

Advancements in Graphics Hardware

The success of WebGL is closely tied to advancements in graphics hardware. Modern GPUs are capable of handling complex rendering tasks, including real-time ray tracing and advanced shading techniques. As hardware continues to improve, the potential for WebGL-based applications to deliver stunning visual experiences will only increase.

The Future of 3D Graphics on the Web

Looking ahead, the future of 3D graphics on the web holds exciting possibilities. Emerging technologies like WebGPU promise even greater performance and cross-platform compatibility. Additionally, the convergence of WebGL with WebXR for mixed reality experiences and WebAssembly for enhanced performance opens up new horizons for web-based 3D content.

In the subsequent chapters of this book, we will explore the capabilities of WebGL in-depth and guide you through the process of harnessing its power to create compelling 3D web experiences.

1.3. Comparing WebGL with Other Graphics Technologies

In this section, we will compare WebGL with other graphics technologies to gain a better understanding of its strengths and weaknesses in the context of web development.

Canvas 2D API

The Canvas 2D API (<canvas>) is a 2D drawing context in HTML5 that allows developers to draw and manipulate graphics on a 2D plane using JavaScript. While it's suitable for rendering 2D graphics, it lacks the capabilities for handling complex 3D scenes. WebGL, on the other hand, is designed explicitly for 3D graphics and provides a more robust solution when 3D visualization is required.

```
// Example of drawing a rectangle on a 2D canvas

const canvas = document.getElementById('myCanvas');

const ctx = canvas.getContext('2d');

ctx.fillStyle = 'blue';

ctx.fillRect(50, 50, 100, 100);
```

Flash

Adobe Flash was once a popular choice for creating interactive multimedia content on the web, including animations and games. However, Flash has become deprecated and is no longer supported by major web browsers due to security concerns and performance issues. WebGL has emerged as a modern replacement for delivering interactive 3D content without the need for plugins.

Unity WebGL

Unity is a popular game development platform that offers WebGL export options. While Unity WebGL allows developers to create highly immersive 3D games and simulations for the web, it often comes with larger file sizes and longer loading times compared to simpler WebGL applications. Unity WebGL is a suitable choice for complex gaming experiences but may not be ideal for lightweight web applications.

```
<!—Example of embedding a Unity WebGL game—>

<iframe src="https://unitywebglgame.com"></iframe>
```

Three.js

Three.js is a JavaScript library that provides a higher-level abstraction for working with WebGL. It simplifies many of the complexities of raw WebGL, making it more accessible for developers. Three.js offers a wide range of features and a robust community, making it an excellent choice for creating 3D web content efficiently.

```
// Example of creating a 3D scene with Three.js

const scene = new THREE.Scene();
```

```
const camera = new THREE.PerspectiveCamera(75, window.innerWidth / window.innerHeight, 0.1, 1000);

const renderer = new THREE.WebGLRenderer();

// ... (additional Three.js code)
```

CSS 3D Transforms

CSS 3D transforms allow developers to apply 3D transformations to HTML elements using CSS properties like transform and perspective. While CSS 3D transforms can add depth and interactivity to web content, they have limitations in terms of complexity and control compared to WebGL. WebGL provides finer-grained control over 3D scenes and is better suited for rendering realistic 3D graphics.

```
/* Example of applying a 3D transformation to a HTML element */

.box {

transform: perspective(500px) rotateX(45deg);

}
```

VRML and X3D

VRML and X3D are previous attempts at bringing 3D graphics to the web but faced limited adoption. They used specialized file formats and often required browser plugins for rendering. WebGL has succeeded in providing a more standardized and plugin-free approach to 3D web graphics.

In summary, WebGL stands out as a powerful and versatile technology for rendering 3D graphics in web browsers. While other technologies may have their merits in specific contexts, WebGL's ability to deliver hardware-accelerated 3D content across modern browsers makes it a go-to choice for developers looking to create immersive web experiences. In the subsequent sections of this book, we'll delve deeper into WebGL's capabilities and how to leverage them effectively.

1.4. Setting Up Your Development Environment

Before diving into WebGL development, it's essential to set up your development environment to ensure a smooth workflow. In this section, we'll guide you through the steps required to prepare your system for WebGL development.

Browser Choice

First and foremost, you'll need a web browser that supports WebGL. Most modern browsers, including Chrome, Firefox, Safari, and Edge, have WebGL support enabled by default. Ensure that you are using an up-to-date version of your preferred browser for the best WebGL experience.

Code Editor

Choose a code editor or integrated development environment (IDE) that you are comfortable with. Popular choices for web development include Visual Studio Code, Sublime Text, Atom, and WebStorm. These editors offer features like code highlighting, autocompletion, and integration with version control systems, making them suitable for WebGL development.

Web Server

To work with WebGL, you'll need a local web server to serve your HTML, JavaScript, and other assets. This is especially important when loading external resources or working with 3D models. You can set up a simple web server using tools like Node.js with the http-server package or Python's built-in http.server. Alternatively, you can use development environments like Create React App or Vue CLI, which come with built-in development servers.

Version Control

Consider using a version control system (VCS) like Git to manage your WebGL projects. Git allows you to track changes, collaborate with others, and easily revert to previous versions if needed. Platforms like GitHub, GitLab, and Bitbucket provide hosting and collaboration features for Git repositories, making it easier to work on projects with a team.

WebGL Debugging Tools

WebGL development often involves debugging complex shaders and graphics code. You can use browser developer tools to inspect and debug your WebGL applications. These tools provide a console for debugging JavaScript code and offer options to examine the WebGL context, shaders, and textures. Familiarize yourself with the developer tools of your chosen browser to streamline the debugging process.

Graphics Drivers

Ensure that your computer's graphics drivers are up-to-date, especially if you plan to work with 3D graphics and WebGL extensively. Updated drivers can provide better performance and compatibility with WebGL applications. Visit your graphics card manufacturer's website to download the latest drivers if necessary.

WebGL Libraries and Frameworks

Consider using WebGL libraries and frameworks to simplify common tasks and accelerate development. Three.js, Babylon.js, and PlayCanvas are popular choices that provide high-level abstractions for working with WebGL. These libraries come with built-in features for creating 3D scenes, handling input, and managing assets.

Testing on Mobile Devices

If you plan to develop WebGL applications for mobile devices, ensure that you have access to a smartphone or tablet for testing. Mobile WebGL performance can vary across devices and browsers, so testing on real hardware is crucial to ensure a smooth user experience.

By setting up your development environment following these guidelines, you'll be well-prepared to start your journey into WebGL development. In the next section, we'll take our first steps by creating a basic WebGL template and exploring the essential components of a WebGL application.

1.5. First Steps: Creating a Basic WebGL Template

Now that you have your development environment set up, it's time to take your first steps into WebGL development by creating a basic WebGL template. In this section, we'll guide you through the process of setting up a minimal WebGL application and explain the essential components.

HTML Structure

Start by creating a new HTML file for your WebGL project. A typical HTML structure for a WebGL application includes the following elements:

```
<!DOCTYPE html>

<html lang="en">

<head>

<meta charset="UTF-8">

<meta name="viewport" content="width=device-width,
initial-scale=1.0">

<title>My WebGL App</title>

</head>

<body>

<canvas id="webgl-canvas"></canvas>

<script src="app.js"></script>

</body>

</html>
```

- The <canvas> element with an id attribute is where we will render our WebGL graphics. It provides a drawing surface for WebGL to work on.

- We include a <script> tag pointing to an external JavaScript file (in this case, "app.js") where we will write our WebGL code.

Setting up the WebGL Context

Next, let's create the "app.js" file and set up the WebGL context. This context is crucial for working with WebGL functions and rendering.

```
// app.js

const canvas = document.getElementById('webgl-canvas');

const gl = canvas.getContext('webgl');

if (!gl) {

console.error('WebGL is not supported in this browser.');

}
```

In this code:

- We retrieve the <canvas> element by its id attribute.
- We obtain the WebGL context by calling getContext('webgl') on the canvas element. If WebGL is not supported in the user's browser, an error message is logged to the console.

Clearing the Canvas

To start with a clean slate, we should clear the canvas to a specific color at the beginning of each frame.

```
// Clear the canvas to black

gl.clearColor(0.0, 0.0, 0.0, 1.0);

gl.clear(gl.COLOR_BUFFER_BIT);
```

Here, we set the clear color to black (RGBA values of 0.0, 0.0, 0.0, and 1.0) and then use gl.clear() to clear the canvas with the specified color.

Creating a Basic Shader Program

To render anything in WebGL, we need to create shader programs. Shaders are small programs executed on the GPU that define how objects are rendered. For now, we'll create a simple shader program that renders a colored triangle.

```
// Vertex shader source code

const vsSource = `

void main() {

gl_Position = vec4(0.0, 0.0, 0.0, 1.0);

}

`;

// Fragment shader source code

const fsSource = `

void main() {

gl_FragColor = vec4(1.0, 0.0, 0.0, 1.0);

}

`;

// Compile the vertex and fragment shaders

const vertexShader = gl.createShader(gl.VERTEX_SHADER);
```

```
gl.shaderSource(vertexShader, vsSource);

gl.compileShader(vertexShader);

const fragmentShader = gl.createShader(gl.FRAGMENT_SHADER);

gl.shaderSource(fragmentShader, fsSource);

gl.compileShader(fragmentShader);

// Create a shader program and link the shaders

const shaderProgram = gl.createProgram();

gl.attachShader(shaderProgram, vertexShader);

gl.attachShader(shaderProgram, fragmentShader);

gl.linkProgram(shaderProgram);

if (!gl.getProgramParameter(shaderProgram, gl.LINK_STATUS)) {

console.error('Unable to initialize the shader program: ' + gl.getProgramInfoLog(shaderProgram));

}
```

In this code:

- We define the source code for a simple vertex shader (vsSource) and fragment shader (fsSource). These shaders are responsible for transforming vertices and defining fragment colors, respectively.
- We compile the shaders, create a shader program, and link the shaders together. We also check for any errors during this process.

Rendering the Triangle

Now, let's render a triangle using our shader program. We'll define the vertices of the triangle and use a buffer to pass the vertex data to the GPU.

```
// Define the vertices of the triangle

const vertices = [

0.0, 1.0, 0.0,

-1.0, -1.0, 0.0,

1.0, -1.0, 0.0

];

// Create a buffer and store the vertex data in it

const vertexBuffer = gl.createBuffer();

gl.bindBuffer(gl.ARRAY_BUFFER, vertexBuffer);

gl.bufferData(gl.ARRAY_BUFFER, new Float32Array(vertices), gl.STATIC_DRAW);

// Get the attribute location and enable it

const positionAttributeLocation = gl.getAttribLocation(shaderProgram, 'a_position');

gl.enableVertexAttribArray(positionAttributeLocation);

gl.vertexAttribPointer(positionAttributeLocation, 3, gl.FLOAT, false, 0, 0);

// Use our shader program for rendering
```

gl.useProgram(shaderProgram);

// Draw the triangle

gl.drawArrays(gl.TRIANGLES, 0, 3);

In this code:

- We define the vertices of a triangle in a JavaScript array.
- We create a buffer (vertexBuffer) to store the vertex data and use gl.bufferData() to upload the data to the GPU.
- We obtain the attribute location for the vertex positions from our shader program and enable it for use.
- We specify how the vertex data is organized (3 values per vertex, of type gl.FLOAT, with no stride) and use the shader program for rendering.
- Finally, we use gl.drawArrays() to render the triangle as a set of triangles.

Running Your WebGL Application

Save your HTML and JavaScript files, and open the HTML file in your web browser. You should see a red triangle displayed on the black canvas.

Congratulations! You've created a basic WebGL template and rendered a simple object. This is just the beginning of your journey into WebGL development. In the upcoming chapters, we'll explore more advanced topics and build exciting 3D web applications.

Chapter 2: Core Concepts of 3D Graphics

2.1. Understanding the 3D Coordinate System

In the world of 3D graphics, understanding the coordinate system is fundamental. It's the foundation upon which all 3D objects are positioned and manipulated. In this section, we'll delve into the 3D coordinate system and its key components.

Cartesian Coordinate System

The most commonly used 3D coordinate system is the Cartesian coordinate system, which is based on three perpendicular axes: X, Y, and Z. These axes intersect at the origin (0, 0, 0). The X-axis typically represents the horizontal direction, the Y-axis represents the vertical direction, and the Z-axis represents the depth or "into the screen" direction.

+Y

|

|

| +Z

| /

| /

| /

| /

```
| /
| /
| / +X
|/_____|
/
/
```

Coordinate Notation

In 3D graphics, we represent points in the 3D space using a notation like (X, Y, Z), where each value represents the position along the respective axis. For example, the point (2, 3, -1) is 2 units to the right (X), 3 units up (Y), and 1 unit behind (negative Z) the origin.

3D Objects

In the 3D coordinate system, objects are defined by their vertices (points in 3D space) and how those vertices connect to create surfaces and shapes. A 3D object can be as simple as a single point or as complex as a highly detailed 3D model.

Transformations

Transformations are fundamental operations in 3D graphics that allow you to move, rotate, and scale objects in 3D space. These transformations are applied to the vertices of an object, altering their positions and orientations. Common transformations include translation (movement), rotation, and scaling.

// Example: Translation transformation

```
const translationMatrix = mat4.create(); // Create a 4x4 transformation matrix

mat4.translate(translationMatrix, translationMatrix, [2.0, 1.0, -1.0]); // Translate by (2, 1, -1)
```

Homogeneous Coordinates

In 3D graphics, we often use homogeneous coordinates, which are a 4D extension of regular Cartesian coordinates. Homogeneous coordinates include an extra dimension (W), and they allow for perspective transformations, such as perspective projection. Homogeneous coordinates are represented as (X, Y, Z, W), and the point (2, 3, -1, 1) is equivalent to (2, 3, -1) in regular Cartesian coordinates.

Viewing and Projection

In 3D rendering, you have to consider the camera's viewpoint and how the 3D scene is projected onto a 2D screen. The viewing transformation determines the camera's position and orientation, while the projection transformation defines how the 3D world is projected onto the 2D viewport. Different projection types, such as perspective and orthographic, result in distinct visual effects.

Understanding the 3D coordinate system is crucial for working with WebGL and 3D graphics in general. It forms the basis for positioning objects, defining camera views, and implementing transformations that bring your 3D scenes to life. In the upcoming sections of this chapter, we'll explore additional core concepts of 3D graphics that will deepen your understanding and proficiency in the field.

2.2. Introduction to Vectors and Matrices

In 3D graphics and WebGL, vectors and matrices are fundamental mathematical constructs used for various operations, including transformations, positioning, and calculations involving 3D objects. Understanding vectors and matrices is crucial for working effectively with 3D graphics. Let's explore these concepts in more detail.

Vectors

A vector is a mathematical object used to represent both direction and magnitude. In 3D graphics, vectors are often used to describe points in space, directions, and transformations. A 3D vector typically consists of three components: X, Y, and Z.

Vector Notation

Vectors are usually represented in column notation as follows:

v=[xyz] =

v=⌊⌈xyz⌋⌉

Where vv is the vector, and xxx, yyy, and zzz are its components along the X, Y, and Z axes, respectively.

Matrices

A matrix is a 2D array of numbers that can represent various linear transformations, such as rotations, scaling, and translations. In 3D graphics, matrices are commonly used to perform transformations on vectors and objects.

Matrix Notation

A 4x4 matrix in 3D graphics is often used to represent transformations and is represented as:

M=[m11m12m13m14m21m22m23m24m31m32m33m34m41m42m4
=

M=⎣⎡m11m21m31m41m12m22m32m42m13m23m33m43m14
m24m34m44⎦⎤

Where mijm_{ij}mij represents the element at the iii-th row and jjj-th column of the matrix.

Vector-Vector Operations

Vectors can be used in various operations, including addition, subtraction, and scalar multiplication. These operations are essential for tasks such as translating objects and calculating surface normals.

Vector Addition

Vector addition involves adding two vectors component-wise:

v1+v2=[x1+x2y1+y2z1+z2]_1 + _2 =

v1+v2=⎣⎡x1+x2y1+y2z1+z2⎦⎤

Vector Subtraction

Vector subtraction is similar to addition but involves subtracting one vector from another:

v1−v2=[x1−x2y1−y2z1−z2]_1 - _2 =

v1−v2=⌊⌈x1−x2y1−y2z1−z2⌋⌉

Scalar Multiplication

Scalar multiplication involves multiplying a vector by a scalar value, which scales the vector:

c·v=[c·xc·yc·z]c =

c·v=⌊⌈c·xc·yc·z⌋⌉

Matrix-Vector Operations

Matrices can also be used to transform vectors. These operations are critical for applying transformations to 3D objects.

Matrix-Vector Multiplication

Matrix-vector multiplication involves multiplying a matrix by a vector to transform the vector:

M·v=[m11m12m13m14m21m22m23m24m31m32m33m34m41m42m4

=

=

M·v=⌊⌈m11m21m31m41m12m22m32m42m13m23m33m43 m14m24m34m44⌋⌉·⌊⌈xyz1⌋⌉=⌊⌈x′y′z′w′⌋⌉

The resulting vector [x′y′z′w′]

⌊⌈x′y′z′w′⌋⌉ represents the transformed point in 3D space.

Matrix-Matrix Operations

Matrices can also be multiplied together to combine transformations.

Matrix Multiplication

Matrix multiplication involves multiplying two matrices to obtain a new matrix. This operation is used to concatenate multiple transformations.

M1·M2=Mresult_1 2 = {}M1·M2=Mresult

Understanding vectors and matrices is crucial for working with 3D graphics. They form the basis for transformations, positioning, and numerous calculations in WebGL and other 3D graphics contexts. In the following sections, we'll explore how these concepts are applied to create and manipulate 3D scenes effectively.

2.3. The Role of Shaders in WebGL

Shaders play a central role in WebGL and 3D graphics in general. They are small programs executed on the GPU (Graphics Processing Unit) that determine how objects are rendered and displayed on the screen. Understanding shaders is crucial for creating custom visual effects and achieving the desired look for your 3D scenes.

Types of Shaders

In WebGL, there are two main types of shaders:

1. Vertex Shader

The vertex shader processes each vertex of a 3D object. Its primary job is to transform the 3D coordinates of the vertices into 2D screen coordinates. This transformation takes into account the camera's position, perspective projection, and any user-defined transformations.

Here's a simplified example of a vertex shader in GLSL (the shader language used in WebGL):

```
// Vertex shader

attribute vec4 a_position;

uniform mat4 u_modelViewProjectionMatrix;

void main() {

// Transform the vertex position

gl_Position = u_modelViewProjectionMatrix * a_position;

}
```

In this example, the a_position attribute represents the vertex's position in 3D space, and the u_modelViewProjectionMatrix is a uniform matrix used to transform the vertex position.

2. Fragment Shader

The fragment shader is responsible for determining the color and appearance of each pixel (fragment) in the rendered image. It can calculate colors based on lighting, textures, and various effects. Fragment shaders are where you can create realistic lighting, simulate materials, and apply post-processing effects.

Here's a simplified example of a fragment shader:

```
// Fragment shader

precision mediump float; // Set the precision for floating-point calculations

void main() {

// Assign a red color to the fragment

gl_FragColor = vec4(1.0, 0.0, 0.0, 1.0);

}
```

In this example, the fragment shader assigns a red color to each fragment, resulting in a red object.

Shader Programs

To use shaders in WebGL, you create shader programs by combining a vertex shader and a fragment shader. These programs define how 3D objects are rendered. Here's a simplified example of creating and using a shader program in WebGL:

```
// Create a shader program

const shaderProgram = gl.createProgram();

// Attach the vertex shader and fragment shader

gl.attachShader(shaderProgram, vertexShader);

gl.attachShader(shaderProgram, fragmentShader);

// Link the shader program

gl.linkProgram(shaderProgram);
```

```
// Use the shader program

gl.useProgram(shaderProgram);
```

Inputs and Outputs

Shaders communicate with each other and the GPU pipeline through inputs and outputs. Vertex shaders typically receive attributes and uniforms as inputs and output the transformed vertex position. Fragment shaders receive interpolated values from the vertex shader and output the final pixel color.

Attributes

Attributes are inputs to the vertex shader and represent per-vertex data, such as vertex positions, normals, and texture coordinates. They are often used to pass data from the CPU to the GPU for processing.

Uniforms

Uniforms are inputs to both vertex and fragment shaders but remain constant for all vertices or fragments during a draw call. They are useful for passing global information like transformation matrices and material properties.

Shader Execution

In WebGL, shaders are executed for each vertex and fragment in parallel on the GPU. This parallelism allows for efficient processing of complex 3D scenes and real-time rendering.

Custom Shaders

One of the strengths of WebGL is the ability to create custom shaders, allowing you to implement unique visual effects and achieve specific rendering styles. You can experiment with different shaders to create realistic lighting, simulate materials, and apply post-processing effects like blurs or distortions.

In summary, shaders are the heart of WebGL and are responsible for transforming 3D data into the final rendered image. Understanding how to write and use shaders is essential for achieving your desired visual results in 3D graphics and WebGL applications. In the following sections of this chapter, we will explore shader languages, debugging, optimization, and creative uses of shaders in more detail.

2.4. Textures and Lighting Basics

Textures and lighting are fundamental aspects of 3D graphics that significantly impact the realism and visual appeal of rendered scenes. In this section, we'll explore the basics of working with textures and lighting in WebGL.

Textures

Textures are 2D images that can be applied to 3D objects to add detail, color, and complexity. They are used to simulate materials like wood, metal, and fabric and can include diffuse colors, specular highlights, and normal maps to enhance the appearance of surfaces.

Texture Coordinates

To map a texture to a 3D object, you need to specify texture coordinates for each vertex of the object. Texture coordinates define how the 2D texture image is projected onto the 3D surface.

Commonly, texture coordinates are represented as (s, t), where (0, 0) corresponds to the bottom-left corner of the texture, and (1, 1) corresponds to the top-right corner.

Texture Filtering

Texture filtering determines how a texture is sampled when mapping it to a 3D object. Two common types of texture filtering are:

- **Nearest-neighbor filtering:** This method selects the nearest texel (texture pixel) to the sample point. It results in blocky and pixelated textures when scaled up or down.

- **Linear filtering:** Linear interpolation between neighboring texels is used to provide smoother transitions between texels. This results in smoother textures when scaled.

Lighting

Lighting in 3D graphics simulates the interaction between light sources and objects in the scene. It influences how objects are illuminated and shaded, giving them depth and realism. WebGL allows you to implement different types of lighting models, including ambient, diffuse, and specular lighting.

Ambient Lighting

Ambient lighting represents the overall illumination of a scene and ensures that objects are visible even in shadowed areas. It provides a base level of brightness to all objects, simulating indirect or bounced light.

Diffuse Lighting

Diffuse lighting represents how light interacts with the surface of an object. It accounts for the direction of the light source and the orientation of the surface, resulting in varying levels of brightness across the surface.

Specular Lighting

Specular lighting simulates the reflection of light off shiny or reflective surfaces. It creates highlights or specular reflections on objects when light sources hit them at specific angles. Specular lighting is used to achieve a glossy or metallic appearance.

Light Sources

In WebGL, you can define various types of light sources, such as point lights, directional lights, and spotlights, to illuminate the scene. Each type of light source has different properties that influence the lighting calculations.

Implementing Textures and Lighting in WebGL

To apply textures and lighting in WebGL, you'll typically need to:

1. Load texture images and bind them to texture units.
2. Pass texture coordinates to the vertex shader to map textures onto 3D objects.
3. Calculate lighting in the fragment shader based on the object's normal vectors, light direction, and material properties.
4. Combine texture colors and lighting calculations to determine the final color of each pixel.

Here's a simplified example of how you might set up textures and basic lighting in WebGL:

```
// Vertex shader

attribute vec4 a_position;

attribute vec2 a_texcoord;

attribute vec3 a_normal;

uniform mat4 u_modelViewProjectionMatrix;

uniform mat4 u_modelViewMatrix;

uniform mat3 u_normalMatrix;

varying vec2 v_texcoord;

varying vec3 v_normal;

void main() {

gl_Position = u_modelViewProjectionMatrix * a_position;

v_texcoord = a_texcoord;

v_normal = normalize(u_normalMatrix * a_normal);

}
```

In the vertex shader, we pass texture coordinates and normals to the fragment shader.

```
// Fragment shader

precision mediump float;

uniform sampler2D u_texture;
```

```
uniform vec3 u_lightDirection;

varying vec2 v_texcoord;

varying vec3 v_normal;

void main() {

// Sample the texture

vec4 texColor = texture2D(u_texture, v_texcoord);

// Calculate diffuse lighting

float diffuse = max(dot(u_lightDirection, v_normal), 0.0);

// Combine texture color and lighting

vec3 resultColor = texColor.rgb * diffuse;

gl_FragColor = vec4(resultColor, texColor.a);

}
```

In the fragment shader, we sample the texture, calculate diffuse lighting, and combine the texture color with lighting to determine the final pixel color.

Texturing and lighting are essential techniques for creating realistic and visually appealing 3D scenes. As you delve deeper into WebGL development, you can explore more advanced lighting models, shadow mapping, and techniques to improve the quality of your rendered graphics.

2.5. Rendering Loops in WebGL

Rendering in WebGL is an iterative process that involves continuously updating the scene and redrawing it on the canvas to create animations and interactive applications. In this section, we'll explore the concept of rendering loops and how they are essential for real-time 3D graphics.

The Rendering Loop

The rendering loop, often referred to as the "game loop" or "main loop," is the core of any interactive 3D application. It's a continuous cycle where the application updates the scene's state and renders it on the screen. The loop typically consists of the following steps:

1. **Input Handling:** Capture user input, such as mouse movements, keyboard presses, or touch events, to control the scene or interact with objects.
2. **Update:** Update the state of the 3D scene. This step includes advancing animations, updating object positions, and processing game logic. It ensures that the scene's data accurately represents the current state of the application.
3. **Rendering:** Render the updated 3D scene onto the canvas. This step involves applying transformations, shaders, textures, and lighting calculations to create the final image.
4. **Display:** Present the rendered image on the screen. This step may involve double buffering or other techniques to prevent flickering or tearing.
5. **Loop:** Repeat the process continuously to maintain real-time interactivity.

The Request Animation Frame API

To create a smooth and efficient rendering loop in modern web applications, it is recommended to use the requestAnimationFrame API provided by most browsers. This API helps synchronize animations with the browser's repaint cycle, resulting in smoother animations and reduced CPU usage.

Here's a simplified example of how to use requestAnimationFrame to create a rendering loop in JavaScript:

```
function renderLoop() {

// Update the scene (e.g., handle user input and update object positions)

updateScene();

// Render the scene

renderScene();

// Request the next frame

requestAnimationFrame(renderLoop);

}

// Start the rendering loop

requestAnimationFrame(renderLoop);
```

In this code:

- The renderLoop function is called recursively using requestAnimationFrame. This ensures that the browser schedules the next frame to be rendered before the current frame is displayed.

- The updateScene function is responsible for updating the scene's state, including handling user input and updating object positions.

- The renderScene function renders the updated scene using WebGL techniques discussed earlier.

Frame Rate and Delta Time

In the context of the rendering loop, it's essential to consider the frame rate (frames per second, or FPS) and delta time (the time elapsed between frames). These parameters affect the smoothness and responsiveness of animations and interactions.

- **Frame Rate:** The frame rate determines how many frames are rendered per second. Common frame rates are 30 FPS, 60 FPS, or higher. A higher frame rate results in smoother animations but may demand more computational resources.

- **Delta Time (Δt):** Delta time represents the time between two consecutive frames. It's often used to update object positions and animations based on the elapsed time. This allows animations to run at consistent speeds regardless of the frame rate.

```
let lastTimestamp = 0;

function renderLoop(timestamp) {

// Calculate delta time

const deltaTime = (timestamp - lastTimestamp) / 1000; // Convert to seconds
```

```
// Update the scene using deltaTime

updateScene(deltaTime);

// Render the scene

renderScene();

// Request the next frame

requestAnimationFrame(renderLoop);

// Store the current timestamp for the next frame

lastTimestamp = timestamp;

}
```

Optimizing the Rendering Loop

Efficient rendering loops are crucial for maintaining good performance in WebGL applications. Some optimization techniques include:

- **Culling:** Only render objects that are within the camera's view frustum. This reduces unnecessary rendering.

- **Batching:** Group objects with the same material and shaders into batches to reduce draw calls.

- **Level of Detail (LOD):** Use lower-polygon models or textures for objects that are far from the camera to improve performance.

- **Frustum Culling:** Exclude objects that are outside the camera's view frustum to avoid unnecessary calculations.

- **Shader and Texture Management:** Minimize shader and texture changes during rendering to improve efficiency.

By optimizing the rendering loop, you can achieve smooth and responsive 3D graphics in your WebGL applications. It's a critical aspect of real-time rendering and interactive experiences. In the following chapters, we'll explore more advanced techniques and features to enhance your WebGL projects.

Chapter 3: Diving into Shaders

3.1. Writing Your First Vertex Shader

Vertex shaders are the starting point for creating 3D graphics in WebGL. They are responsible for transforming the 3D coordinates of vertices into 2D screen coordinates. In this section, we'll dive into the basics of writing your first vertex shader in WebGL.

Shader Basics

Before we get into writing code, let's understand the basic structure of a shader. A shader program in WebGL consists of two main components: a vertex shader and a fragment shader. The vertex shader is responsible for transforming vertex positions, while the fragment shader deals with pixel colors.

Here's a simplified template of a WebGL shader program:

```
// Vertex Shader

attribute vec4 a_position;

uniform mat4 u_modelViewProjectionMatrix;

void main() {

// Transform the vertex position

gl_Position = u_modelViewProjectionMatrix * a_position;

}

// Fragment Shader

precision mediump float;
```

```
void main() {
// Set the pixel color
gl_FragColor = vec4(1.0, 0.0, 0.0, 1.0); // Red color
}
```

In this template:

- The vertex shader receives a vertex position (a_position) and a transformation matrix (u_modelViewProjectionMatrix) as inputs. It calculates the transformed position (gl_Position) that represents the vertex in screen space.

- The fragment shader sets the pixel color (gl_FragColor) for each pixel in the fragment. In this example, it sets the color to red.

Shader Language (GLSL)

Shaders in WebGL are written in GLSL (OpenGL Shading Language), which is a C-like language designed for writing graphics shaders. GLSL provides a rich set of data types, functions, and features for performing various operations in the shaders.

Vertex Attributes and Uniforms

- **Attributes:** Attributes are inputs to the vertex shader and represent per-vertex data, such as vertex positions, normals, and texture coordinates. In the template, a_position is an example of an attribute.

- **Uniforms:** Uniforms are inputs to both the vertex and fragment shaders but remain constant for all vertices or fragments during a draw call. They are used for passing global information like transformation matrices and material properties. In the template, u_modelViewProjectionMatrix is an example of a uniform.

The main() Function

The main() function is the entry point of both the vertex and fragment shaders. It is executed for each vertex (in the vertex shader) or each pixel (in the fragment shader). Inside main(), you perform the necessary calculations to achieve the desired output.

Writing Your First Vertex Shader

Let's write a simple vertex shader that moves a 3D object along the X-axis. This shader will translate the object's vertices by a specified amount.

```
// Vertex Shader

attribute vec4 a_position;

uniform mat4 u_modelMatrix;

void main() {

// Translate the vertex along the X-axis

vec4 newPosition = u_modelMatrix * a_position;

gl_Position = newPosition;

}
```

In this shader:

- We receive the vertex position as a_position and a model matrix as u_modelMatrix.
- Inside main(), we calculate the new position by multiplying the model matrix with the vertex position.
- Finally, we assign the new position to gl_Position, which represents the transformed vertex position.

This simple vertex shader demonstrates the concept of transforming vertices using a model matrix. You can build upon this foundation to create more complex vertex shaders that implement various transformations and effects.

3.2. Exploring Fragment Shaders

Fragment shaders are a crucial component of WebGL and 3D graphics, responsible for determining the color and appearance of each pixel (fragment) in the rendered image. In this section, we'll explore fragment shaders, their role, and how to write and use them effectively.

Role of Fragment Shaders

Fragment shaders come into play after the vertex shader has transformed 3D vertices into 2D screen coordinates. Their primary responsibility is to calculate the final color of each pixel on the screen. This calculation can involve various factors, such as lighting, texturing, materials, and post-processing effects.

Example Use Cases:

- **Lighting:** Fragment shaders can calculate the effects of ambient, diffuse, and specular lighting to create realistic illumination on surfaces.
- **Texturing:** They can sample textures and apply them to objects, giving them detailed appearances and textures.
- **Materials:** Fragment shaders can simulate various materials like metals, glass, or wood by modifying how light interacts with surfaces.
- **Post-Processing:** After rendering the scene, fragment shaders can apply post-processing effects like blurs, color corrections, and depth of field.

Shader Language (GLSL)

Like vertex shaders, fragment shaders are written in GLSL (OpenGL Shading Language). GLSL provides a rich set of functions, data types, and operations for performing calculations in shaders.

The main() Function

The main() function in a fragment shader is the entry point where calculations are performed for each pixel. Inside main(), you can access various inputs and perform operations to determine the final pixel color.

Inputs in Fragment Shaders

Fragment shaders receive several inputs that are crucial for calculating pixel colors:

- **Varyings:** Varyings are variables that are interpolated across the primitive (triangle) from the vertex shader to the fragment shader. They allow you to pass data from the vertex shader to the fragment shader smoothly.

- **Uniforms:** Uniforms are constants that remain the same for all pixels in a draw call. They are typically used to pass global data, such as transformation matrices and material properties, from the CPU to the GPU.

- **Samplers:** Samplers are used to access textures in fragment shaders. They allow you to sample texture data and apply it to objects in the scene.

Writing Your First Fragment Shader

Let's write a simple fragment shader that renders a solid color for each pixel. This shader will receive a uniform color and apply it to all fragments.

```
// Fragment Shader

precision mediump float;

uniform vec4 u_color; // Uniform for the color

void main() {

// Set the pixel color to the uniform color

gl_FragColor = u_color;

}
```

In this shader:

- We receive a uniform color (u_color) as an input.

- Inside main(), we directly assign the uniform color to gl_FragColor, which represents the final pixel color.

This basic fragment shader renders all pixels in the specified uniform color. It serves as a starting point for more complex fragment shaders that involve lighting, texturing, and material simulations.

Implementing Texturing in Fragment Shaders

One common use case for fragment shaders is texturing. To apply textures to objects, you sample texture data in the fragment shader and blend it with other shading calculations. Here's an example of how to implement texture mapping in a fragment shader:

```
// Fragment Shader with Texture

precision mediump float;

uniform sampler2D u_texture; // Uniform for the texture

varying vec2 v_texcoord; // Varying for texture coordinates

void main() {

// Sample the texture using texture coordinates

vec4 texColor = texture2D(u_texture, v_texcoord);

// Set the pixel color to the sampled texture color

gl_FragColor = texColor;

}
```

In this shader:

- We receive a uniform sampler2D (u_texture) for the texture and a varying (v_texcoord) for the texture coordinates. The varying is typically passed from the vertex shader.

- Inside main(), we sample the texture using the texture2D() function, which takes the uniform texture and the varying texture coordinates as inputs.

- We assign the sampled texture color to gl_FragColor, which gives us the final pixel color.

This fragment shader applies the sampled texture to each pixel, allowing you to create detailed and textured 3D objects.

Fragment shaders are essential for controlling the appearance of objects in your WebGL applications. As you delve deeper into 3D graphics, you can explore more advanced fragment shader techniques for realistic lighting, material simulations, and post-processing effects.

3.3. Shader Languages: GLSL Essentials

GLSL (OpenGL Shading Language) is the primary language used for writing shaders in WebGL and OpenGL-based graphics programming. In this section, we'll explore the essentials of GLSL, its syntax, data types, and key concepts.

Shader Basics

GLSL is a C-like language designed specifically for writing graphics shaders. Shaders are small programs that run on the GPU (Graphics Processing Unit) and determine how 3D objects are rendered. There are two main types of shaders in GLSL:

- **Vertex Shaders:** Responsible for transforming 3D coordinates of vertices into 2D screen coordinates.

- **Fragment Shaders:** Determine the color and appearance of each pixel (fragment) in the rendered image.

Shader Structure

A GLSL shader program consists of the following sections:

- **Version Declaration:** Specifies the version of GLSL being used. For example, #version 300 es indicates version 3.00 for WebGL.

- **Input and Output Declarations:** Define the inputs and outputs of the shader. Vertex shaders typically receive attributes and uniforms, while fragment shaders have varyings and can set gl_FragColor as the output.

- **Main Function:** Contains the shader's main logic, where calculations are performed for each vertex (in vertex shaders) or each pixel (in fragment shaders).

Data Types

GLSL provides various data types for performing calculations and storing data. Some common data types include:

- **Scalars:** float (single-precision floating-point number), int (integer), bool (boolean).

- **Vectors:** vec2, vec3, vec4 (2D, 3D, and 4D vectors of floats).

- **Matrices:** mat2, mat3, mat4 (2x2, 3x3, and 4x4 matrices of floats).

- **Textures:** sampler2D (for 2D textures), samplerCube (for cube maps).

Operators

GLSL supports a wide range of operators for performing arithmetic, logical, and comparison operations. Some common operators include:

- Arithmetic: +, -, *, /, %.

- Logical: &&, ||, !.

- Comparison: ==, !=, <, >, <=, >=.

Functions

GLSL provides built-in functions for common operations like vector and matrix manipulation, trigonometry, and more. For example, dot(), cross(), normalize(), sin(), cos(), abs(), and mix() are commonly used functions.

Control Flow

GLSL supports conditional statements (if, else, switch) and loops (for, while, do-while) for control flow. However, complex control flow is often discouraged in shaders due to their parallel execution nature on the GPU.

Precision Qualifiers

GLSL allows you to specify the precision of floating-point calculations using precision qualifiers. Common precision qualifiers include highp (high precision), mediump (medium precision), and lowp (low precision). Precision qualifiers can impact the performance and accuracy of shader calculations.

Comments

Comments in GLSL are similar to C-style comments and can be single-line (//) or multi-line (/* */). They are used to document code and improve readability.

Example Shader

Here's a simplified example of a GLSL shader that calculates the dot product of two vectors and sets the output color based on the result:

```
#version 300 es

precision mediump float;

// Input vectors

uniform vec3 u_vectorA;

uniform vec3 u_vectorB;

void main() {

// Calculate the dot product

float dotProduct = dot(u_vectorA, u_vectorB);

// Set the output color based on the dot product

gl_FragColor = vec4(vec3(dotProduct), 1.0);

}
```

In this shader:

- We specify the GLSL version and precision qualifier.

- Two uniform vectors u_vectorA and u_vectorB are received as inputs.

- Inside the main() function, we calculate the dot product of the input vectors and set the output color based on the result.

Understanding GLSL is essential for writing and customizing shaders in WebGL and OpenGL-based applications. It provides the foundation for creating complex rendering effects, simulations, and interactive graphics. As you delve deeper into shader programming, you can explore more advanced GLSL features and techniques to enhance your 3D graphics.

3.4. Debugging and Optimizing Shaders

Debugging and optimizing shaders are crucial steps in the development of WebGL and OpenGL-based graphics applications. In this section, we'll explore techniques for debugging and optimizing shaders to ensure they perform efficiently and produce the desired results.

Debugging Shaders

Debugging shaders can be challenging because they run on the GPU, making traditional debugging tools less effective. However, there are some strategies you can employ to identify and fix shader issues:

1. **Shader Errors:** Check the console for shader compilation errors. Shader compilation errors are reported by the WebGL API and can help you identify syntax errors or other issues in your shader code.

2. **Visual Debugging:** Use visual techniques to debug shaders. For example, you can render intermediate values as colors to visualize calculations or highlight specific parts of your scene to identify rendering issues.
3. **Uniform and Varying Values:** Print the values of uniforms and varyings in your shader to inspect their values during shader execution. This can help you pinpoint problems related to data passing between shaders.
4. **Shader Preambles:** Create shader preambles or separate functions for complex calculations. This makes it easier to isolate and debug specific parts of your shader code.
5. **Shader Analyzers:** Some third-party tools and libraries provide shader analysis and debugging features. These tools can help you visualize shader execution and identify performance bottlenecks.

Optimizing Shaders

Shader optimization is essential for achieving smooth and efficient rendering in 3D graphics applications. Here are some optimization techniques for shaders:

1. **Minimize Calculations:** Reduce the number of calculations in your shader by eliminating unnecessary operations and using simplified expressions where possible. Avoid redundant calculations.
2. **Loop Unrolling:** Unroll loops in your shader to remove loop control overhead. This can improve shader performance, especially on mobile devices.
3. **Texture Sampling:** Optimize texture sampling by using lower-resolution textures for objects that are distant or small on the screen. Implement texture mipmapping for smoother transitions between different levels of detail.

4. **Use Built-In Functions:** Take advantage of built-in GLSL functions for common operations like normalization, vector dot products, and trigonometric functions. These functions are often optimized by the GPU driver.
5. **Avoid Branching:** Minimize conditional branching in your shader code, as it can lead to divergent execution paths on the GPU, reducing performance.
6. **Reduce Memory Access:** Minimize memory access in shaders, especially in fragment shaders. Accessing uniforms and textures can be costly, so use them sparingly.
7. **Batching:** Group objects with the same materials and shaders into batches to reduce draw calls and shader switches.
8. **Shader LOD:** Implement Level of Detail (LOD) techniques to adjust shader complexity based on the object's distance from the camera.
9. **Profiling:** Use profiling tools to identify shader bottlenecks and performance issues. Profiling can help you pinpoint areas that require optimization.
10. **GPU Vendor-Specific Optimizations:** Be aware that different GPU vendors may have specific optimizations or quirks. Testing on various hardware can help you identify platform-specific performance improvements.

Shader Compilation and Caching

In WebGL, shader compilation can be expensive in terms of both time and resources. To improve performance, consider the following:

1. **Precompile Shaders:** Precompile shaders on the CPU and cache the compiled shader programs. This avoids runtime compilation delays and reduces GPU load.

2. **Shader Minification:** Minify your shader code to reduce its size. Smaller shaders load faster and can lead to improved performance.
3. **Dynamic Shader Loading:** Load shaders dynamically when needed rather than all at once. This can reduce the initial loading time of your application.
4. **Shader Caching:** Implement a shader caching mechanism to reuse compiled shaders across different parts of your application.

By debugging and optimizing your shaders, you can ensure that your WebGL or OpenGL-based graphics application runs efficiently and produces high-quality visuals. Balancing visual quality and performance is a critical aspect of 3D graphics development, and careful attention to shaders plays a significant role in achieving this balance.

3.5. Creative Uses of Shaders in WebGL

Shaders in WebGL are not limited to the traditional tasks of rendering objects and applying lighting. They offer a wide range of creative possibilities for enhancing visuals and creating unique effects in your 3D graphics. In this section, we'll explore some creative uses of shaders beyond the basics.

Post-Processing Effects

One of the most common creative uses of shaders is applying post-processing effects to the rendered scene. Post-processing shaders can alter the final image in various ways, such as adding blurs, color grading, bloom, vignetting, and more.

Here's a simple example of a post-processing fragment shader that applies a grayscale effect to the entire scene:

```
// Fragment Shader for Grayscale Effect

precision mediump float;

uniform sampler2D u_texture; // Uniform for the scene's texture

void main() {

// Sample the scene's texture

vec4 color = texture2D(u_texture, gl_FragCoord.xy / u_resolution.xy);

// Convert to grayscale by taking the average of RGB channels

float gray = (color.r + color.g + color.b) / 3.0;

// Set the pixel color to grayscale

gl_FragColor = vec4(vec3(gray), 1.0);

}
```

This shader takes the rendered scene's texture, calculates the grayscale value for each pixel, and sets the pixel color to grayscale. Post-processing shaders like this can dramatically change the visual style of your application.

Simulations and Visual Effects

Shaders can be used to create simulations and visual effects, ranging from realistic physics simulations to abstract and artistic visuals. Here are some examples:

- **Water Simulation:** Shaders can simulate realistic water surfaces with ripples, reflections, and refractions.

- **Fire and Smoke:** Create dynamic and animated fire and smoke effects using shaders.

- **Particle Systems:** Shaders are often used to render thousands of particles with varying properties like size, color, and behavior.

- **Procedural Generation:** Generate procedural textures, terrain, and structures using shaders.

- **Fractals and Kaleidoscopes:** Create mesmerizing visual patterns and fractals using recursive shaders.

Image and Video Manipulation

Shaders are powerful tools for image and video manipulation. You can use them to apply filters, transformations, and artistic effects to images and videos in real-time. This is particularly useful for applications that involve webcam input, live streaming, or photo editing.

Non-Photorealistic Rendering (NPR)

Non-Photorealistic Rendering techniques use shaders to create artistic and stylized visuals that resemble traditional art forms. Examples include cel-shading to achieve a cartoon-like appearance, hatching and stippling for a hand-drawn look, or ink and watercolor effects.

Creative Animations

Shaders can be used to create captivating animations that go beyond typical 3D animations. For example, you can simulate dynamic backgrounds, generate mesmerizing patterns, or create abstract animations that respond to user interactions.

Interactive Experiences

Shaders can enhance user interaction by responding to mouse movements, clicks, or other input events. For instance, you can create interactive 3D objects that change appearance or behavior based on user actions, providing engaging and immersive experiences.

Audio-Visual Experiences

Combining shaders with audio input can result in stunning audio-visual experiences. You can synchronize visuals with music beats, visualize sound waves, or create interactive audio-visual installations.

Augmented Reality (AR) and Virtual Reality (VR)

In AR and VR applications, shaders play a significant role in creating immersive environments, rendering virtual objects, and applying effects that enhance the user's perception of the virtual world.

These creative uses of shaders demonstrate the versatility and potential for innovation in WebGL and OpenGL-based graphics programming. By pushing the boundaries of shader development, you can create unique and visually compelling experiences that captivate your audience and stand out in the world of 3D graphics.

Chapter 4: Advanced Rendering Techniques

4.1. Implementing Shadow Mapping

Shadow mapping is a widely used technique in 3D graphics to create realistic shadows cast by objects in a scene. Shadows add depth and realism to the rendered images. In this section, we'll explore the concept of shadow mapping and how to implement it in WebGL.

The Importance of Shadows

Shadows are crucial for creating a sense of depth and realism in 3D scenes. They help viewers perceive the relative positions of objects and the interaction of light with the environment. Implementing shadows in WebGL can significantly enhance the visual quality of your 3D applications.

Shadow Mapping Overview

Shadow mapping is a technique that simulates the casting of shadows in a 3D scene by rendering the scene from the perspective of a light source and storing depth information in a shadow map. This shadow map is then used to determine whether a point in the scene is in shadow or not when rendering the final image from the camera's perspective.

The basic steps involved in shadow mapping are as follows:

1. **Shadow Map Generation:** Render the scene from the perspective of the light source to create a depth map, known as the shadow map. The shadow map stores the distance from the light source to each point in the scene.

2. **Shadow Map Sampling:** During the final rendering pass, sample the shadow map for each fragment to determine the distance from the fragment to the light source. This distance is then compared to the value stored in the shadow map.
3. **Shadow Testing:** If the distance from the fragment to the light source is greater than the distance stored in the shadow map, the fragment is in shadow. Otherwise, it is lit.
4. **Shadow Softening:** To create soft shadows, you can introduce techniques like percentage-closer filtering (PCF) or variance shadow mapping.

Implementing Shadow Mapping in WebGL

Implementing shadow mapping in WebGL involves several steps:

1. **Creating the Shadow Map:** Set up a framebuffer and a texture to store the depth values from the light's perspective. Render the scene from the light's point of view to populate the shadow map.
2. **Shadow Map Sampling:** In the final rendering pass, sample the shadow map for each fragment. Calculate the depth from the fragment to the light source and compare it to the depth stored in the shadow map.
3. **Shadow Testing:** Determine whether the fragment is in shadow based on the depth comparison. Adjust the fragment's color or intensity accordingly.
4. **Shadow Softening (Optional):** To create soft shadows, you can apply techniques like PCF or Gaussian blur to the shadow map sampling.

Here's a simplified example of a fragment shader that performs shadow mapping:

// Fragment Shader with Shadow Mapping

precision mediump float;

uniform sampler2D u_colorTexture; *// Uniform for the scene's color texture*

uniform sampler2D u_shadowMap; *// Uniform for the shadow map*

varying vec4 v_shadowCoord; *// Varying for shadow map coordinates*

void main() {

// Calculate the depth from the fragment to the light source

float fragDepth = v_shadowCoord.z / v_shadowCoord.w;

// Sample the shadow map

float shadowDepth = texture2D(u_shadowMap, v_shadowCoord.xy).r;

// Perform the shadow test

float shadow = fragDepth > shadowDepth ? 0.5 : 1.0;

// Sample the scene's color texture

vec4 color = texture2D(u_colorTexture, gl_TexCoord[0].xy);

// Combine color with shadow factor

gl_FragColor = color * shadow;

}

In this shader:

- We calculate the depth from the fragment to the light source using the shadow map coordinates.
- We sample the shadow map to retrieve the depth stored in the shadow map at the fragment's position.
- The shadow test is performed by comparing the fragment's depth to the shadow map depth. If the fragment's depth is greater, it's in shadow; otherwise, it's lit.
- Finally, we combine the fragment's color with the shadow factor to apply shadows.

Implementing shadow mapping can be complex, but it significantly enhances the visual quality of your 3D scenes. With shadow mapping, you can create realistic and dynamic shadows that add depth and realism to your WebGL applications.

4.2. Exploring Bump and Normal Mapping

Bump and normal mapping are techniques used in computer graphics to simulate intricate surface details and enhance the realism of 3D objects without increasing their geometric complexity. These techniques are particularly useful for creating the illusion of fine textures, bumps, and imperfections on surfaces. In this section, we'll explore bump and normal mapping and how to implement them in WebGL.

The Need for Surface Detail

In 3D graphics, representing fine surface details on objects can be computationally expensive due to the increased polygon count required for complex geometries. Bump and normal mapping provide a solution to this problem by faking the appearance of detailed surfaces without adding more polygons.

Normal Mapping

Normal mapping is the most common technique for simulating surface details. It relies on a texture map called a normal map, where each pixel stores a normal vector that describes the orientation of the surface at that point. These normal vectors are used during rendering to perturb the lighting calculations, creating the illusion of surface bumps and crevices.

Here's how normal mapping works in WebGL:

1. **Normal Map Creation:** Create a normal map that encodes the surface normals of the 3D object. This is typically done in specialized 3D modeling software or generated procedurally.
2. **Normal Map Texturing:** During rendering, sample the normal map for each fragment of the object. The sampled normal vector is then used in lighting calculations.
3. **Lighting Calculation:** Modify the lighting calculations (e.g., Phong or Blinn-Phong shading) by taking the sampled normal into account. This results in light interacting with the object as if it had surface details.

```
// Fragment Shader with Normal Mapping

precision mediump float;

uniform sampler2D u_colorTexture; // Uniform for the scene's color texture

uniform sampler2D u_normalMap; // Uniform for the normal map
```

```
varying vec2 v_texCoord; // Varying for texture coordinates

void main() {

// Sample the color texture

vec4 color = texture2D(u_colorTexture, v_texCoord);

// Sample the normal map

vec3 normal = texture2D(u_normalMap, v_texCoord).xyz;

// Transform the normal from [0, 1] range to [-1, 1]

normal = normalize(normal * 2.0 - 1.0);

// Perform lighting calculations using the modified normal

// ...

// Combine color with lighting calculations

gl_FragColor = vec4(color.rgb * lighting, color.a);

}
```

Bump Mapping

Bump mapping is a similar technique to normal mapping, but it uses a grayscale heightmap texture instead of a normal map. The heightmap encodes the surface's height variations, and these variations are used to perturb the surface normals during rendering.

Here's a simplified example of bump mapping in WebGL:

1. **Heightmap Creation:** Create a grayscale heightmap that represents the surface details of the object.
2. **Heightmap Texturing:** Sample the heightmap for each

fragment during rendering.

3. **Normal Perturbation:** Perturb the surface normal based on the heightmap value. This simulates the bumpiness of the surface.
4. **Lighting Calculation:** Perform lighting calculations considering the perturbed normals.

Bump and normal mapping are valuable techniques for adding visual richness to 3D objects while maintaining efficient geometry. These methods are commonly used in video games, simulations, and computer-generated imagery (CGI) to create realistic surfaces and intricate textures on a wide range of objects.

4.3. Particle Systems in WebGL

Particle systems are a fundamental technique in computer graphics used to simulate a wide range of natural phenomena such as fire, smoke, rain, and explosions. In WebGL, particle systems can add dynamism and realism to 3D scenes by representing these phenomena as collections of small, individually controlled particles. In this section, we'll explore the concept of particle systems and how to implement them in WebGL.

Particle Systems Overview

A particle system is composed of multiple small particles that move and interact independently to create complex visual effects. Each particle has properties like position, velocity, color, size, and lifespan. These properties are typically updated over time to simulate various behaviors.

Creating a Particle System

Implementing a particle system in WebGL involves several steps:

1. **Particle Initialization:** Create and initialize a pool of particles with random or predefined properties. Set their initial positions, velocities, colors, sizes, and lifespans.
2. **Particle Update:** In each frame of the animation loop, update the properties of each particle based on its behavior. For example, you can update positions based on velocities, change colors to simulate fading or blending, and decrement lifespans.
3. **Rendering:** Render each particle as a small 2D or 3D object. Particles are typically rendered as points, quads, or textured sprites. Apply transformations to position and orient particles in 3D space.
4. **Particle Recycling:** When particles reach the end of their lifespans or exit the visible scene, recycle them by resetting their properties and placing them back in the available pool. This avoids creating new particles continuously.

Example: Implementing a Simple Particle System

Here's a simplified example of a particle system in WebGL. This example demonstrates how to create a basic particle system that simulates falling snowflakes.

```
// Define a Particle class to represent individual particles

class Particle {

constructor() {

this.position = vec3.create();

this.velocity = vec3.fromValues(0, -0.02, 0); // Falling velocity

this.size = Math.random() * 0.1 + 0.05; // Random size
```

```
this.color = [1, 1, 1, 1]; // White color
this.lifespan = Math.random() * 500 + 100; // Random lifespan
}
update() {
// Update position based on velocity
vec3.add(this.position, this.position, this.velocity);
// Decrease lifespan
this.lifespan—;
}
}
// Create an array to store particles
const particles = [];
// Initialize the particle system
function initParticleSystem() {
for (let i = 0; i < 1000; i++) {
particles.push(new Particle());
}
}
// Update and render the particle system in the animation loop
function updateAndRenderParticles() {
```

```
for (let i = 0; i < particles.length; i++) {
const particle = particles[i];
particle.update();
// Render the particle (e.g., as a point or sprite)
renderParticle(particle);
// Recycle particles that have reached the end of their lifespan
if (particle.lifespan <= 0) {
// Reset particle properties and position it at the top
particle.position[0] = Math.random() * 10 - 5; // Random x position
particle.position[1] = 5; // Y position at the top
particle.position[2] = Math.random() * 10 - 5; // Random z position
particle.velocity[1] = -0.02; // Reset velocity
particle.size = Math.random() * 0.1 + 0.05; // Random size
particle.color = [1, 1, 1, 1]; // Reset color
particle.lifespan = Math.random() * 500 + 100; // Random lifespan
}
}
}
```

This code snippet demonstrates the fundamental structure of a particle system, including particle initialization, updating, rendering, and recycling. In a real application, you would also need to integrate this with your WebGL rendering pipeline to achieve the desired visual effects.

Particle systems are versatile and can be adapted to simulate a wide range of natural phenomena and dynamic effects in your WebGL applications, adding depth and realism to your 3D scenes.

4.4. Real-time Environment Reflections

Real-time environment reflections, often referred to as screen-space reflections (SSR), are a rendering technique used to simulate the reflection of objects in a 3D scene based on the environment and other objects present. SSR can greatly enhance the realism of 3D graphics by accurately reflecting the surroundings and dynamically changing as the camera and objects move. In this section, we'll explore the concept of real-time environment reflections and how to implement them in WebGL.

The Importance of Reflections

Reflections play a vital role in the visual fidelity of 3D scenes. They contribute to the perception of materials, lighting, and spatial relationships. Realistic reflections provide depth and immersion, making the virtual world feel more believable.

SSR Algorithm Overview

Screen-space reflections work by capturing the scene's surroundings from the camera's perspective and using that information to determine what should be reflected on surfaces. Here are the basic steps involved:

1. **Reflection Ray Generation:** For each pixel on the screen, trace a reflection ray in the direction opposite to the

camera's view. This ray represents a virtual camera viewing the scene from the reflection point.

2. **Intersection Testing:** Determine where the reflection ray intersects with objects in the scene. This is done using techniques like ray tracing or ray marching.
3. **Reflection Sampling:** Once the intersection point is found, sample the surrounding environment or other objects to determine the reflected color and intensity.
4. **Blending:** Combine the reflected color with the original material properties of the surface. This can involve techniques like Fresnel blending to mimic material properties.
5. **Rendering:** Render the final scene with reflections added to the surfaces, providing the illusion of reflective materials.

Implementing SSR in WebGL

Implementing SSR in WebGL can be complex due to the need for ray tracing or ray marching. Here's a simplified overview of the process:

1. **Reflection Ray Generation:** For each pixel, calculate the reflection ray direction based on the camera's view and the surface normal at that pixel.
2. **Intersection Testing:** Trace the reflection ray to find intersections with objects in the scene. This can be achieved through techniques like ray-plane or ray-sphere intersection tests.
3. **Reflection Sampling:** Sample the environment or objects at the intersection point to obtain the reflected color and intensity. This involves sampling textures or other relevant data.

4. **Blending:** Combine the reflected color with the surface's original color using blending equations, taking into account material properties and Fresnel effects.
5. **Rendering:** Render the final scene with the reflection data added to the surfaces.

Implementing SSR in WebGL may require advanced shader programming and can be computationally intensive. Additionally, handling dynamic scenes and multiple reflective surfaces can add complexity to the implementation. However, the visual impact of accurate reflections on the realism of your 3D scenes is well worth the effort.

Note that real-time environment reflections can also be implemented using techniques like cube mapping and screen-space reflection probes, which are computationally less expensive but may not provide the same level of accuracy as ray tracing-based methods. The choice of technique depends on the desired level of realism and performance considerations.

4.5. Post-processing Effects

Post-processing effects are a powerful tool in 3D graphics and WebGL for enhancing the visual quality and style of a scene after the initial rendering is complete. These effects are applied as a final step in the rendering pipeline, allowing you to manipulate the colors, depth, and overall appearance of the image. In this section, we'll explore the concept of post-processing effects in WebGL and how to implement them to achieve various visual enhancements.

Post-processing in the Rendering Pipeline

In the traditional rendering pipeline, post-processing effects are applied to the rendered image in a separate pass. This involves taking the final frame and processing it with a series of shaders, each responsible for a specific effect. These shaders manipulate the pixel data, depth information, and other properties of the image to achieve the desired visual outcome.

Common Post-processing Effects

1. **Color Grading:** Adjust the colors and tones of the image to achieve a specific look or mood. This can involve changing the brightness, contrast, saturation, and applying color filters.
2. **Bloom:** Create a halo or glow effect around bright objects in the scene, simulating the effect of intense light sources.
3. **Depth of Field (DOF):** Simulate the blur that occurs in the foreground and background of a camera's focus point. This effect adds realism and can direct the viewer's attention.
4. **Motion Blur:** Add motion blur to fast-moving objects in the scene to create a sense of speed and fluidity.
5. **Anti-aliasing:** Improve the quality of edges and reduce jaggedness in the image by applying anti-aliasing techniques.
6. **Vignetting:** Darken the corners of the image to draw attention to the center, creating a cinematic or dramatic effect.
7. **Lens Distortion:** Simulate lens imperfections, such as barrel distortion or chromatic aberration, for a more authentic and unique look.

Implementing Post-processing Effects

To implement post-processing effects in WebGL, you'll typically use a framebuffer to render the scene to a texture. Then, you can apply a series of fragment shaders to this texture to achieve the desired effects. Here's a simplified example of a post-processing effect that adds a bloom effect to a scene:

```
// Bloom Fragment Shader

precision mediump float;

uniform sampler2D u_sceneTexture; // Scene texture

varying vec2 v_texCoord; // Varying for texture coordinates

void main() {

vec4 color = texture2D(u_sceneTexture, v_texCoord);

// Apply bloom effect (example: increase brightness)

color.rgb += 0.5;

gl_FragColor = color;

}
```

In this example, we sample the scene texture and apply a simple brightness increase as a bloom effect. In a real application, you would use more complex shaders and techniques to achieve various post-processing effects.

Post-processing effects are a versatile tool for enhancing the visual quality and style of your WebGL applications. They can be used to create cinematic, stylized, or realistic looks, and they allow for creative experimentation and artistic expression in 3D graphics. By combining multiple post-processing effects, you can achieve visually stunning results and create immersive experiences for your users.

Chapter 5: 3D Models and Animation

5.1. Importing 3D Models into WebGL

Importing 3D models into WebGL is a fundamental aspect of creating interactive and immersive 3D web applications. 3D models bring life to your scenes, allowing you to represent objects, characters, and environments with high fidelity. In this section, we'll explore the process of importing 3D models into WebGL and incorporating them into your projects.

The Importance of 3D Models

3D models are essential in 3D graphics because they serve as the visual representation of objects and entities in your scenes. Whether you're building a game, simulation, or visualization, 3D models are the building blocks that enable you to create complex and realistic environments.

Popular 3D Model Formats

Before you can use 3D models in WebGL, you need to choose a suitable file format. Some popular 3D model formats compatible with WebGL include:

- **Wavefront OBJ:** A simple and widely supported format that stores 3D geometry and materials. It is text-based and can be easily parsed.

- **GLTF (GL Transmission Format):** A binary format that supports complex 3D scenes, materials, animations, and more. GLTF is becoming increasingly popular for web-based 3D graphics due to its efficiency.

• **FBX (Filmbox):** Developed by Autodesk, FBX is a versatile format that can store 3D models, animations, and scene hierarchy. It's commonly used in game development.

• **Collada (DAE):** An XML-based format that supports not only 3D geometry but also animations, materials, and scene information. Collada files can be converted for use in WebGL.

Loading 3D Models in WebGL

To load 3D models in WebGL, you'll typically use a 3D modeling library or framework that provides functions for parsing and rendering models. Three.js is one of the most popular libraries for this purpose. Here's a simplified example of how to load a 3D model using Three.js:

```
// Import Three.js library

import * as THREE from 'three';

// Create a scene and camera

const scene = new THREE.Scene();

const camera = new THREE.PerspectiveCamera(75, window.innerWidth / window.innerHeight, 0.1, 1000);

camera.position.z = 5;

// Create a WebGLRenderer

const renderer = new THREE.WebGLRenderer();

renderer.setSize(window.innerWidth, window.innerHeight);
```

```
document.body.appendChild(renderer.domElement);

// Load a 3D model (GLTF format)

const loader = new THREE.GLTFLoader();

loader.load('path/to/model.gltf', (gltf) => {

const model = gltf.scene;

scene.add(model);

});

// Create an animation loop

const animate = () => {

requestAnimationFrame(animate);

// Rotate the model or perform other animations here

renderer.render(scene, camera);

};

animate();
```

In this example, we use Three.js to create a scene, load a GLTF format 3D model, and render it. You can manipulate the loaded model and add animations to bring it to life within your WebGL application.

Importing 3D models is a crucial step in creating engaging and interactive 3D web experiences. With the right tools and libraries, you can seamlessly integrate 3D models into your WebGL projects, opening up a world of possibilities for creative and immersive web applications.

5.2. Basics of 3D Model Animation

Animating 3D models in WebGL adds life and interactivity to your scenes, making them dynamic and engaging. Whether you're creating games, simulations, or interactive visualizations, understanding the basics of 3D model animation is essential. In this section, we'll explore the fundamental concepts of animating 3D models in WebGL.

Key Concepts in 3D Model Animation

Before delving into the implementation, let's clarify some key concepts:

- **Keyframes:** Animation in 3D models is often achieved by specifying keyframes at specific points in time. A keyframe defines the state of the model's transformation (position, rotation, scale) at that time.

- **Interpolation:** To smoothly transition between keyframes, interpolation techniques are used. Linear interpolation (lerp) and spherical linear interpolation (slerp) are common methods for interpolating position and rotation.

- **Skeletons and Bones:** For character animation, a skeleton composed of bones is often used. Each bone has its transformation, and the movement of the bones influences the mesh attached to them.

- **Blend Shapes:** Blend shapes, also known as morph targets or shape keys, are used to deform the mesh to create facial expressions or other deformations.

Animating Position and Rotation

Animating the position and rotation of a 3D model involves specifying keyframes for these transformations over time. Here's a simplified example using Three.js:

```
// Create a model

const model = new THREE.Object3D();

scene.add(model);

// Define keyframes for position and rotation

const positionKeyframes = [

{ time: 0, position: new THREE.Vector3(0, 0, 0) },

{ time: 1, position: new THREE.Vector3(0, 2, 0) },

{ time: 2, position: new THREE.Vector3(0, 0, 0) },

];

const rotationKeyframes = [

{ time: 0, rotation: new THREE.Euler(0, 0, 0) },

{ time: 1, rotation: new THREE.Euler(0, Math.PI, 0) },

{ time: 2, rotation: new THREE.Euler(0, 0, 0) },

];

// Create animation clips

const positionClip = new THREE.AnimationClip('position', -1, positionKeyframes);
```

```
const rotationClip = new THREE.AnimationClip('rotation', -1, rotationKeyframes);

// Create an animation mixer

const mixer = new THREE.AnimationMixer(model);

// Add the clips to the mixer

mixer.clipAction(positionClip).play();

mixer.clipAction(rotationClip).play();

// Animate the model in the render loop

const animate = () => {

requestAnimationFrame(animate);

mixer.update(0.01); // Update the animation mixer

renderer.render(scene, camera);

};

animate();
```

In this example, we create keyframes for position and rotation and use Three.js's animation system to blend between these keyframes over time. The mixer.update function advances the animation.

Character Animation with Skeletons

Character animation often involves skeletons and bones. The model's mesh is skinned to the skeleton, allowing it to deform realistically. Here's a simplified example:

```
// Create a skinned character
```

```
const character = new THREE.SkinnedMesh(geometry, material);
scene.add(character);
// Create a skeleton and bones
const skeleton = new THREE.Skeleton(bones);
character.bind(skeleton); // Bind the mesh to the skeleton
// Define keyframes for bone rotations
const boneKeyframes = [
{ time: 0, rotations: [0, 0, 0] },
{ time: 1, rotations: [Math.PI / 4, 0, 0] },
{ time: 2, rotations: [0, 0, 0] },
];
// Create an animation clip for bones
const boneClip = new THREE.AnimationClip('bones', -1, boneKeyframes);
// Create an animation mixer for bones
const boneMixer = new THREE.AnimationMixer(character);
// Add the bone clip to the mixer
boneMixer.clipAction(boneClip).play();
// Animate the character in the render loop
const animate = () => {
requestAnimationFrame(animate);
```

```
boneMixer.update(0.01); // Update the bone animation mixer

renderer.render(scene, camera);

};

animate();
```

In this example, we use a skeleton and bones to deform the character's mesh. The keyframes specify rotations for individual bones.

Animating 3D models in WebGL allows you to create dynamic and interactive experiences. Whether it's simple transformations or complex character animations, understanding the basics of 3D model animation is crucial for bringing your 3D scenes to life.

5.3. Skeletal Versus Frame-Based Animation

When it comes to animating 3D models in WebGL and other 3D graphics applications, you have two primary approaches: skeletal animation and frame-based animation. Each method has its strengths and use cases, and understanding the differences between them is essential for choosing the right animation technique for your project. In this section, we'll explore both skeletal and frame-based animation and discuss their advantages and limitations.

Skeletal Animation

Skeletal animation, also known as rigging, is a popular technique for animating character models and other deformable 3D objects. It relies on a hierarchical structure of bones (or joints) that deform the mesh attached to them. Here's how skeletal animation works:

- **Skeleton:** A skeleton is composed of a hierarchy of bones connected in a tree-like structure. Each bone has its transformation (position and rotation).

- **Skinning:** The 3D model's mesh is associated with the skeleton. Each vertex in the mesh is influenced by one or more bones, which control its position and deformation. This is achieved through weighted vertex blending.

- **Keyframes:** Animations are created by specifying keyframes for the positions and rotations of the bones. Interpolation is used to smoothly transition between keyframes.

Advantages of Skeletal Animation:

1. Realistic Deformation: Skeletal animation allows for realistic deformation of characters and objects, making it suitable for character animations and organic shapes.
2. Efficient: It is memory-efficient because it only stores bone transformations and weights per vertex, rather than storing the position of each vertex for each frame.
3. Interactivity: Skeletal animation can be interactive, allowing characters to respond to user input in real-time.

Limitations of Skeletal Animation:

1. Complex Setup: Setting up a skeleton and weight painting can be time-consuming, especially for complex characters.
2. Limited to Deformable Objects: Skeletal animation is best suited for objects that can be deformed using bones. It may not be suitable for non-deformable objects or rigid body animations.

Frame-Based Animation

Frame-based animation, also known as keyframe animation or frame-by-frame animation, is a straightforward technique where each frame of an animation is explicitly defined. Here's how frame-based animation works:

- **Keyframes:** Animations are created by specifying the complete state of the 3D model (position, rotation, and possibly other properties) for each frame.

- **Linear Interpolation:** Transitions between keyframes are achieved through linear interpolation. The computer calculates intermediate frames by blending between adjacent keyframes.

Advantages of Frame-Based Animation:

1. Simplicity: Frame-based animation is easy to understand and set up, making it suitable for simple animations.
2. Fine Control: You have full control over each frame, allowing for precise and artistic control over the animation.
3. Suitable for Non-Deformable Objects: Frame-based animation can be used for non-deformable objects, such as cameras, lights, or rigid body animations.

Limitations of Frame-Based Animation:

1. Memory Intensive: Storing the complete state of the 3D model for each frame can be memory-intensive, especially for long animations or complex scenes.
2. Limited Interactivity: Frame-based animations are typically pre-rendered and played back as videos or sequences, limiting interactivity in real-time applications.

Choosing the Right Animation Technique

The choice between skeletal and frame-based animation depends on your project's requirements. For character animations and deformable objects, skeletal animation is the preferred choice due to its realism and efficiency. Frame-based animation is better suited for non-deformable objects, simple animations, or situations where fine control over each frame is necessary.

In many cases, a combination of both techniques may be used within a single project to leverage the strengths of each method where they are most appropriate. Ultimately, the choice of animation technique should align with your project's goals and the desired level of realism and interactivity.

5.4. Interactive Animation Techniques

Interactive animation in WebGL allows users to actively engage with 3D content, creating a dynamic and immersive experience. Unlike pre-defined animations, interactive animations respond to user input in real-time, enabling user-driven exploration and interaction. In this section, we'll explore various techniques for implementing interactive animations in WebGL.

User Input and Event Handling

To create interactive animations, you need to capture user input and respond to events such as mouse clicks, keyboard presses, touch gestures, and more. WebGL applications typically rely on JavaScript event handlers to detect and respond to user input.

Here's a simple example of using event listeners to respond to a mouse click:

```
// Detect a mouse click on a 3D object
renderer.domElement.addEventListener('click', (event) => {
const mouse = new THREE.Vector2();
mouse.x = (event.clientX / window.innerWidth) * 2 - 1;
mouse.y = -(event.clientY / window.innerHeight) * 2 + 1;
const raycaster = new THREE.Raycaster();
raycaster.setFromCamera(mouse, camera);
// Check for intersections with 3D objects
const intersects = raycaster.intersectObjects(scene.children);
if (intersects.length > 0) {
// Handle the click on an object
const clickedObject = intersects[0].object;
// Perform animations or interactions based on the click
}
});
```

In this example, we use the Three.js library to detect mouse clicks on 3D objects within the scene and respond accordingly. Similar event handling techniques can be applied to other user input events.

Animation Control

Interactive animations often involve controlling the behavior and state of 3D objects based on user input. You can achieve this by manipulating object properties, such as position, rotation, and scale, in response to user actions.

Here's a basic example of how to move a 3D object in response to keyboard input:

```
// Detect keyboard input

document.addEventListener('keydown', (event) => {

const speed = 0.1; // Adjust the movement speed

switch (event.key) {

case 'ArrowUp':

// Move the object forward

object.position.z -= speed;

break;

case 'ArrowDown':

// Move the object backward

object.position.z += speed;

break;

case 'ArrowLeft':

// Move the object to the left

object.position.x -= speed;

break;

case 'ArrowRight':
```

```
// Move the object to the right

object.position.x += speed;

break;

}

});
```

In this example, we detect arrow key presses and update the position of a 3D object accordingly. You can apply similar principles to control other aspects of your interactive animations, such as rotation, scaling, or triggering specific animations.

Animation Transitions

Interactive animations often involve smooth transitions between different states or poses. You can achieve this by using techniques like interpolation (lerp or slerp) to smoothly transition from one state to another based on user input or events.

Here's a simplified example of interpolating the rotation of a 3D object to create a smooth animation:

```
// Smoothly interpolate the rotation of an object

function animateRotation(targetRotation, duration) {

const initialRotation = object.rotation.clone();

const startTime = Date.now();

function animate() {

const currentTime = Date.now();

const elapsedTime = currentTime - startTime;
```

```
const t = Math.min(elapsedTime / duration, 1);

object.rotation.lerp(targetRotation, t);

if (t < 1) {

requestAnimationFrame(animate);

}

}

animate();

}
```

In this example, the animateRotation function smoothly interpolates the rotation of the object from its current state to a target rotation over a specified duration.

User Interface (UI) Elements

To enhance the interactivity of your WebGL applications, you can incorporate user interface (UI) elements such as buttons, sliders, and menus. These UI elements can be used to control animations, change scenes, or adjust parameters in real-time.

Libraries like dat.GUI can help you create interactive UI components that allow users to customize and control your WebGL animations with ease.

Interactive animations in WebGL provide a dynamic and engaging user experience, allowing users to actively interact with 3D content. By capturing user input, controlling animations, transitioning smoothly between states, and incorporating user interface elements, you can create captivating interactive WebGL applications that respond to user actions in real-time.

5.5. Working with Animation Libraries

Creating complex animations from scratch in WebGL can be challenging, especially for intricate and detailed movements. To simplify the animation development process, many developers turn to animation libraries and frameworks that provide pre-built tools and features for handling animations. In this section, we'll explore the advantages of using animation libraries in WebGL and introduce some popular options.

Advantages of Animation Libraries

Using animation libraries in WebGL offers several advantages:

1. **Ease of Use:** Animation libraries often provide high-level abstractions that make it easier to create complex animations with minimal code.
2. **Cross-Browser Compatibility:** Libraries are typically designed to work consistently across different web browsers, saving you from dealing with browser-specific issues.
3. **Efficiency:** Many libraries are optimized for performance, ensuring smooth animations even in resource-intensive scenarios.
4. **Rich Features:** Libraries often include features such as tweening, easing functions, timelines, and more, making it easier to create sophisticated animations.

Popular Animation Libraries

Let's take a look at some popular animation libraries for WebGL:

1. Three.js AnimationSystem

Three.js[1] is a widely used 3D graphics library that includes a built-in animation system. It provides support for keyframe animations, morph target animations, and skeletal animations. Three.js makes it relatively straightforward to animate 3D objects and scenes. Here's a simple example of how to create a basic animation using Three.js:

```
const geometry = new THREE.BoxGeometry();

const material = new THREE.MeshBasicMaterial({ color: 0x00ff00 });

const cube = new THREE.Mesh(geometry, material);

scene.add(cube);

const animation = new THREE.AnimationMixer(cube);

const clip = THREE.AnimationClip.CreateFromMorphTargetSequence('blink', geometry.morphAttributes.position, 30);

animation.clipAction(clip).play();
```

2. GreenSock Animation Platform (GSAP)

GSAP is a robust animation library that can be used for both 2D and 3D animations. While it's not WebGL-specific, it provides powerful tools for creating complex animations and is often used alongside WebGL frameworks. GSAP offers features like tweening, timelines, and a wide range of easing functions.

```
// Example using GSAP to animate a 3D object's rotation
```

1. https://threejs.org/

```
gsap.to(cube.rotation, { duration: 2, x: Math.PI / 2, y: Math.PI / 2,
z: Math.PI / 2, repeat: -1, yoyo: true });
```

3. Anime.js

Anime.js[2] is a lightweight JavaScript animation library that specializes in creating smooth and performant animations. While primarily designed for 2D animations, it can be integrated with WebGL projects to animate HTML elements or 2D overlays within a 3D scene.

```
// Example using Anime.js to animate an HTML element

anime({

targets: '#myElement',

translateX: 250,

rotate: '1turn',

backgroundColor: '#FFF',

duration: 2000,

loop: true,

});
```

4. PixiJS

PixiJS[3] is a versatile 2D rendering engine that is often used in combination with WebGL for 2D and 3D game development and

2. https://animejs.com/

3. https://pixijs.com/

interactive animations. It provides a powerful and flexible platform for creating interactive content.

```
// Example using PixiJS to animate a sprite

const sprite = new PIXI.Sprite(texture);

sprite.position.set(0, 0);

app.stage.addChild(sprite);

const animation = gsap.to(sprite, { x: 300, duration: 2, repeat: -1, yoyo: true });
```

These animation libraries can significantly simplify the animation development process in WebGL. Depending on your specific project requirements and familiarity with the library, you can choose the one that best suits your needs and workflow. Incorporating an animation library can save you time and effort, allowing you to focus on creating engaging and interactive animations for your WebGL applications.

Chapter 6: User Interaction and Events 6.1. Capturing Mouse and Keyboard Input 6.2. Implementing Touch Controls 6.3. Creating Interactive 3D Objects 6.4. Collision Detection Basics 6.5. Building an Interactive 3D Interface

---

Chapter 6: User Interaction and Events

6.1. Capturing Mouse and Keyboard Input

In WebGL applications, user interaction plays a crucial role in creating immersive and engaging experiences. Capturing mouse and keyboard input allows you to enable users to interact with 3D objects, control cameras, trigger animations, and more. In this section, we will explore how to capture mouse and keyboard input in WebGL and use it to enhance user interaction within your 3D scenes.

Handling Mouse Input

Capturing mouse input is fundamental for user interaction in WebGL. You can detect various mouse events such as clicks, mouse movements, and scrolling to trigger specific actions within your 3D scene.

Here's an example of how to capture a mouse click event using JavaScript and WebGL:

```
// Detect a mouse click on the WebGL canvas

renderer.domElement.addEventListener('click', (event) => {

// Convert mouse coordinates to 3D world coordinates

const mouse = new THREE.Vector2(

(event.clientX / window.innerWidth) * 2 - 1,

-(event.clientY / window.innerHeight) * 2 + 1

);
```

```
// Create a raycaster to check for intersections with 3D objects
const raycaster = new THREE.Raycaster();
raycaster.setFromCamera(mouse, camera);
// Find intersections with objects in the scene
const intersects = raycaster.intersectObjects(scene.children);
if (intersects.length > 0) {
// Handle the click on an object
const clickedObject = intersects[0].object;
// Perform actions or animations based on the click
}
});
```

In this example, we add an event listener to the WebGL canvas to detect mouse clicks. When a click occurs, we convert the 2D mouse coordinates to 3D world coordinates using a raycaster. Then, we check for intersections between the ray and 3D objects in the scene. If there is an intersection, we can perform actions or trigger animations on the clicked object.

Handling Keyboard Input

Keyboard input is another essential aspect of user interaction. It allows users to control objects, navigate scenes, and perform various actions within your WebGL application.

Here's a basic example of how to capture keyboard input using JavaScript and WebGL:

```
// Detect keyboard input
document.addEventListener('keydown', (event) => {
// Check the key code to determine which key was pressed
switch (event.key) {
case 'ArrowUp':
// Handle the "ArrowUp" key press (e.g., move an object forward)
break;
case 'ArrowDown':
// Handle the "ArrowDown" key press (e.g., move an object backward)
break;
case 'ArrowLeft':
// Handle the "ArrowLeft" key press (e.g., rotate an object left)
break;
case 'ArrowRight':
// Handle the "ArrowRight" key press (e.g., rotate an object right)
break;
default:
// Handle other key presses if needed
break;
}
```

```
});
```

In this example, we add an event listener to the document to detect keyboard input. When a key is pressed, we check the key code to determine which key was pressed and respond accordingly. Depending on the key press, you can implement various actions, such as moving, rotating, or triggering specific behaviors in your WebGL scene.

Combining Mouse and Keyboard Input

To create more interactive experiences, you can combine mouse and keyboard input to enable users to control multiple aspects of your WebGL application simultaneously. For example, you can use mouse input to interact with 3D objects and use keyboard input for navigation or camera control.

```
// Example combining mouse and keyboard input

document.addEventListener('keydown', (event) => {

switch (event.key) {

case 'ArrowUp':

// Handle the "ArrowUp" key press (e.g., move the camera forward)

break;

case 'ArrowDown':

// Handle the "ArrowDown" key press (e.g., move the camera backward)

break;

// Handle other key presses for camera control or other actions
```

```
}
});
renderer.domElement.addEventListener('click', (event) => {
const mouse = new THREE.Vector2(
(event.clientX / window.innerWidth) * 2 - 1,
-(event.clientY / window.innerHeight) * 2 + 1
);
const raycaster = new THREE.Raycaster();
raycaster.setFromCamera(mouse, camera);
const intersects = raycaster.intersectObjects(scene.children);
if (intersects.length > 0) {
const clickedObject = intersects[0].object;
// Handle object interactions based on the click
}
});
```

By combining mouse and keyboard input, you can create more dynamic and user-friendly WebGL applications that respond to user actions effectively. Whether you're building games, simulations, or interactive data visualizations, capturing user input is essential for providing engaging and interactive experiences within your 3D scenes.

6.2. Implementing Touch Controls

In the modern era of web development, many users access web applications and WebGL content on touch-enabled devices such as smartphones and tablets. Therefore, it's crucial to implement touch controls to provide an optimal user experience on these devices. In this section, we will explore how to implement touch controls in your WebGL applications.

Detecting Touch Events

To enable touch controls, you need to detect and respond to touch events. JavaScript provides touch event handlers that allow you to capture various touch-related interactions, including tapping, swiping, pinching, and dragging.

Here's an example of how to detect and respond to touch events in WebGL using JavaScript:

```
// Detect a touch start event on the WebGL canvas

renderer.domElement.addEventListener('touchstart', (event) => {

// Get the first touch point

const touch = event.touches[0];

// Capture the initial touch position

const startX = touch.clientX;

const startY = touch.clientY;

// Handle touch start, e.g., initiate an action

});
```

```
// Detect a touch move event on the WebGL canvas

renderer.domElement.addEventListener('touchmove', (event) => {

// Get the first touch point

const touch = event.touches[0];

// Capture the current touch position

const currentX = touch.clientX;

const currentY = touch.clientY;

// Calculate the distance moved or perform actions based on touch movement

});

// Detect a touch end event on the WebGL canvas

renderer.domElement.addEventListener('touchend', (event) => {

// Handle touch end, e.g., finalize an action

});
```

In this example, we add event listeners for touchstart, touchmove, and touchend events on the WebGL canvas. When a user touches the screen, the touchstart event is triggered, allowing you to capture the initial touch position. As the user moves their finger, the touchmove event is fired, enabling you to track touch movement and respond accordingly. Finally, when the user releases their touch, the touchend event can be used to finalize actions or animations.

Handling Multi-Touch

Many touch-enabled devices support multi-touch interactions, allowing users to use multiple fingers simultaneously. To support multi-touch in your WebGL application, you can expand your touch event handling to accommodate multiple touch points.

```
// Detect a touch start event on the WebGL canvas

renderer.domElement.addEventListener('touchstart', (event) => {

// Loop through all active touch points

for (let i = 0; i < event.touches.length; i++) {

const touch = event.touches[i];

// Capture touch information for each point

const touchX = touch.clientX;

const touchY = touch.clientY;

// Handle touch start for each touch point

}

});

// Detect a touch move event on the WebGL canvas

renderer.domElement.addEventListener('touchmove', (event) => {

// Loop through all active touch points

for (let i = 0; i < event.touches.length; i++) {

const touch = event.touches[i];
```

```
// Capture touch information for each point
const touchX = touch.clientX;
const touchY = touch.clientY;
// Handle touch move for each touch point
}
});
// Detect a touch end event on the WebGL canvas
renderer.domElement.addEventListener('touchend', (event) => {
// Loop through all active touch points
for (let i = 0; i < event.touches.length; i++) {
const touch = event.touches[i];
// Handle touch end for each touch point
}
});
```

By iterating through all active touch points, you can track and respond to multi-touch interactions effectively. This allows you to implement gestures and actions that involve multiple fingers, providing a more immersive experience on touch-enabled devices.

Gesture Libraries

For complex multi-touch gestures like pinch-to-zoom or two-finger rotation, you can consider using JavaScript libraries specifically designed for touch gestures, such as Hammer.js. These libraries simplify the implementation of gestures and provide a higher level of abstraction for touch-based interactions.

```
// Example of using Hammer.js for pinch-to-zoom gesture
const hammertime = new Hammer(renderer.domElement);
hammertime.get('pinch').set({ enable: true });
hammertime.on('pinch', (event) => {
const scale = event.scale; // Get the pinch scale value
// Implement zooming or scaling based on the pinch gesture
});
```

In this example, Hammer.js is used to handle pinch-to-zoom gestures. The library abstracts the touch events and provides a convenient way to detect and respond to such gestures.

Implementing touch controls in your WebGL application is essential for ensuring a seamless and intuitive user experience on touch-enabled devices. Whether you're creating games, 3D simulations, or interactive data visualizations, touch controls can greatly enhance the accessibility and usability of your web content.

6.3. Creating Interactive 3D Objects

Interactivity is a key aspect of engaging WebGL applications. While capturing user input and implementing touch controls are essential, creating interactive 3D objects within your scenes adds another layer of immersion and user engagement. In this section, we will explore how to make your 3D objects interactive by responding to user interactions.

Object Interaction Basics

Interactive 3D objects can respond to user actions such as clicks, mouse hover, or touch events. To create interactive objects, you'll typically use libraries like Three.js to handle object selection and interaction.

Here's a basic example of how to make a 3D object clickable using Three.js:

```
// Create a clickable 3D object

const clickableObject = new THREE.Mesh(geometry, material);

scene.add(clickableObject);

// Detect a mouse click event on the WebGL canvas

renderer.domElement.addEventListener('click', (event) => {

const mouse = new THREE.Vector2(

(event.clientX / window.innerWidth) * 2 - 1,

-(event.clientY / window.innerHeight) * 2 + 1

);

const raycaster = new THREE.Raycaster();

raycaster.setFromCamera(mouse, camera);

const intersects = raycaster.intersectObject(clickableObject);

if (intersects.length > 0) {

// The object was clicked

// Perform actions or trigger animations on the object
```

```
}
});
```

In this example, we create a clickable 3D object and add it to the scene. When a user clicks on the WebGL canvas, we use a raycaster to check if the click intersects with the clickable object. If there's an intersection, we can respond to the click event by performing actions or triggering animations on the object.

Interactive 3D Buttons

One common use case for interactive 3D objects is creating buttons within your WebGL application. These buttons can trigger actions or navigate to different parts of your 3D scene.

Here's a simplified example of how to create an interactive 3D button using Three.js:

```
// Create a button as a clickable 3D object

const buttonGeometry = new THREE.BoxGeometry(1, 0.2, 0.2);

const buttonMaterial = new THREE.MeshBasicMaterial({ color: 0x00ff00 });

const button = new THREE.Mesh(buttonGeometry, buttonMaterial);

scene.add(button);

// Position the button in 3D space

button.position.set(0, 1, -2);

// Detect a mouse click event on the WebGL canvas
```

```
renderer.domElement.addEventListener('click', (event) => {
const mouse = new THREE.Vector2(
(event.clientX / window.innerWidth) * 2 - 1,
-(event.clientY / window.innerHeight) * 2 + 1
);
const raycaster = new THREE.Raycaster();
raycaster.setFromCamera(mouse, camera);
const intersects = raycaster.intersectObject(button);
if (intersects.length > 0) {
// The button was clicked
// Perform actions or navigation based on the button click
}
});
```

In this example, we create a 3D button as a clickable object and position it in the scene. When the user clicks on the button, we use the raycaster to check for intersections, and if the button is clicked, we can execute actions or navigate to other parts of the scene.

Advanced Interactions

Beyond simple clicks, you can implement more advanced interactions such as object dragging, resizing, or rotation. These interactions can be achieved by capturing user input (mouse or touch events) and updating the object's properties accordingly.

```
// Example of object dragging using mouse events
let isDragging = false;
clickableObject.addEventListener('mousedown', () => {
isDragging = true;
});
document.addEventListener('mousemove', (event) => {
if (isDragging) {
// Update the object's position based on mouse movement
const deltaX = event.movementX;
const deltaY = event.movementY;
clickableObject.position.x += deltaX * 0.01;
clickableObject.position.y -= deltaY * 0.01;
}
});
document.addEventListener('mouseup', () => {
isDragging = false;
});
```

In this example, we allow the user to drag the object by capturing mouse events. When the user clicks on the object, dragging is enabled, and we update the object's position based on mouse movement. When the user releases the mouse button, dragging is disabled.

Creating interactive 3D objects opens up a wide range of possibilities for your WebGL applications. Whether it's creating buttons, draggable objects, or interactive elements within data visualizations, user interaction with 3D objects can greatly enhance the user experience and make your application more engaging.

6.4. Collision Detection Basics

Collision detection is a fundamental aspect of creating interactive 3D environments in WebGL. It allows you to determine when two or more objects in your scene intersect or collide with each other. This section explores the basics of collision detection in WebGL and provides an overview of common techniques and libraries used to implement it.

Why Collision Detection Matters

Collision detection is essential for a variety of applications, from gaming and simulations to data visualization and interactive 3D modeling. It enables you to create realistic interactions between objects, detect user interactions, and implement physics simulations.

For example, in a game, collision detection is used to check if a player character collides with obstacles, enemies, or collectible items. In a data visualization application, it can be used to determine if a user's pointer intersects with a specific data point or chart element, triggering interactions.

Basic Collision Detection Techniques

1. **Bounding Boxes**: One of the simplest collision detection techniques involves using bounding boxes or bounding spheres. Each object is enclosed in a simple geometric shape (e.g., a box or sphere), and collision detection checks

if these shapes intersect. While not the most accurate method, it is efficient and suitable for many applications.

2. **Raycasting**: Raycasting involves sending a ray (a line with an origin and direction) from one object and checking if it intersects with another object. This method is commonly used for picking or selecting objects in 3D scenes based on user input. When the ray intersects with an object, it implies a collision.
3. **Mesh Collision**: In this approach, the 3D geometry of objects is analyzed for collision. More complex than bounding boxes, it provides precise collision detection but can be computationally expensive for detailed meshes. Libraries like Three.js offer mesh-based collision detection.

Here's a simplified example of bounding box collision detection using Three.js:

```
// Assuming obj1 and obj2 are your 3D objects

const box1 = new THREE.Box3().setFromObject(obj1);

const box2 = new THREE.Box3().setFromObject(obj2);

if (box1.intersectsBox(box2)) {

// Collision detected between obj1 and obj2

// Handle the collision here

}
```

Using Physics Engines

For more complex simulations and gaming applications, using physics engines like Cannon.js or Ammo.js can simplify collision detection and response. These engines provide advanced features like rigid body physics, constraints, and accurate collision detection.

For instance, you can simulate realistic physics interactions such as object bouncing, rolling, or sliding, and accurately detect collisions between objects with complex shapes.

Optimization and Performance

Efficient collision detection is crucial for smooth real-time applications. To optimize performance, consider techniques like spatial partitioning (e.g., Octrees or BVH) to reduce the number of collision checks. Additionally, you can implement collision layers and filters to specify which objects should or shouldn't collide.

In conclusion, collision detection is a vital component of interactive 3D applications. Whether you're creating games, simulations, or data visualization tools, understanding the basics of collision detection and choosing the right technique or library for your project is essential for creating engaging and responsive WebGL experiences.

6.5. Building an Interactive 3D Interface

Creating an interactive 3D interface is an exciting endeavor that allows you to design immersive user experiences. In this section, we'll explore the process of building interactive 3D interfaces in WebGL, covering the key concepts and techniques involved.

Designing the User Interface

Before diving into the technical aspects, it's essential to plan and design your 3D interface. Consider the following:

1. **User Interaction**: Determine how users will interact with

the interface. Will they use mouse and keyboard controls, touch gestures, or virtual reality (VR) controllers? Design the interface to be intuitive and user-friendly.

2. **Layout and Placement**: Decide where and how 3D elements will be positioned within the scene. Consider the spatial relationships between objects and how users will navigate the interface.
3. **Feedback and Animation**: Think about how the interface will provide feedback to user actions. Animation and visual cues can enhance the user experience and guide interactions.

Implementing Interactive Elements

3D Objects as UI Elements

In WebGL, you can use 3D objects as interactive UI elements. For example, buttons can be represented as 3D objects that users can click on or interact with using gestures.

Here's a simplified example of creating a clickable 3D button using Three.js:

```
// Create a 3D button as a clickable object

const buttonGeometry = new THREE.BoxGeometry(1, 0.2, 0.2);

const buttonMaterial = new THREE.MeshBasicMaterial({ color: 0x00ff00 });

const button = new THREE.Mesh(buttonGeometry, buttonMaterial);

scene.add(button);
```

```
// Position the button in 3D space
button.position.set(0, 1, -2);
// Detect a mouse click event on the WebGL canvas
renderer.domElement.addEventListener('click', (event) => {
const mouse = new THREE.Vector2(
(event.clientX / window.innerWidth) * 2 - 1,
-(event.clientY / window.innerHeight) * 2 + 1
);
const raycaster = new THREE.Raycaster();
raycaster.setFromCamera(mouse, camera);
const intersects = raycaster.intersectObject(button);
if (intersects.length > 0) {
// The button was clicked
// Perform actions or navigation based on the button click
}
});
```

User Feedback and Animation

Interactive interfaces often rely on feedback and animations to provide context and guide users. You can use techniques like tweening and keyframe animations to create smooth transitions and visual cues.

For instance, when a user hovers over a 3D button, you can animate its scale to indicate interactivity. Three.js provides animation tools and libraries for implementing these effects.

```
// Add a hover effect to the button

button.addEventListener('mouseenter', () => {

// Animate the button's scale to indicate interactivity

new TWEEN.Tween(button.scale)

.to({ x: 1.1, y: 1.1, z: 1.1 }, 200)

.start();

});

button.addEventListener('mouseleave', () => {

// Restore the button's original scale

new TWEEN.Tween(button.scale)

.to({ x: 1, y: 1, z: 1 }, 200)

.start();

});
```

Navigation and Interaction Patterns

Consider the navigation and interaction patterns you want to implement in your 3D interface. This could include:

- **Point-and-Click Navigation**: Allowing users to click on objects to trigger actions or move to different scenes.

- **Gesture-Based Interaction**: Implementing gestures for zooming, rotating, or scaling 3D elements.

- **VR Controller Support**: Supporting virtual reality controllers for immersive interactions in VR environments.

Performance and Optimization

Building an interactive 3D interface can be resource-intensive. To ensure smooth performance, optimize your code, use level-of-detail techniques for complex scenes, and handle textures and shaders efficiently.

Additionally, consider implementing occlusion culling to avoid rendering objects that are not currently visible to the user, further improving performance.

In summary, building an interactive 3D interface in WebGL involves careful planning, designing interactive elements, providing user feedback, and optimizing performance. By following best practices and leveraging libraries like Three.js, you can create captivating and engaging 3D user experiences.

7.1. Combining WebGL with HTML Elements

In this section, we will explore the integration of WebGL content with HTML elements to create interactive and dynamic 3D graphics that can be seamlessly embedded within web pages. Combining WebGL and HTML allows developers to build immersive user interfaces and incorporate 3D visualizations into their web applications.

HTML and WebGL Synergy

The integration of WebGL and HTML is a powerful technique that leverages the strengths of both technologies. HTML provides the structure and user interface elements, while WebGL handles the rendering of complex 3D scenes and graphics.

Here are some common scenarios where combining HTML and WebGL is beneficial:

1. **User Interface Elements**: You can place HTML buttons, forms, and other interface elements around or on top of your WebGL canvas. This allows users to interact with your 3D content using familiar HTML controls.
2. **Information Overlay**: Display dynamic information or tooltips on HTML elements that appear when the user interacts with 3D objects. This helps in providing context and enhancing user understanding.
3. **Responsive Design**: By using HTML and CSS, you can create responsive designs that adapt to various screen sizes and orientations, ensuring your WebGL content is accessible on both desktop and mobile devices.

Overlaying HTML Elements on WebGL

To overlay HTML elements on top of a WebGL canvas, you can use the CSS position property with a value of absolute or relative. Here's an example of overlaying an HTML button on a WebGL canvas:

```
<div style="position: relative;">

<canvas id="webglCanvas"></canvas>

<button style="position: absolute; top: 10px; left: 10px;">Click Me</button>

</div>
```

In this example, the div containing the WebGL canvas and the button is set to position: relative, and the button is set to position: absolute. This positions the button relative to the div container, allowing you to control its placement.

Communicating Between HTML and WebGL

To create interactions between HTML elements and WebGL content, you can use JavaScript. For instance, you can add event listeners to HTML elements that trigger actions in your WebGL code.

```
const button = document.querySelector('#myButton');

const canvas = document.querySelector('#webglCanvas');

button.addEventListener('click', () => {

// Perform actions or trigger animations in your WebGL code

// based on the button click
```

```
});

// You can also communicate from WebGL to HTML by modifying HTML elements:

function updateHTMLText(text) {

const infoElement = document.querySelector('#infoElement');

infoElement.textContent = text;

}
```

Responsive Design

Creating a responsive design for your WebGL content ensures that it looks good and functions well across various devices and screen sizes. Utilize CSS media queries to adapt the layout and scaling of HTML and WebGL elements based on the device's characteristics.

```
@media (max-width: 768px) {

/* Adjust CSS styles for smaller screens */

#webglCanvas {

width: 100%;

height: 300px;

}

}
```

By combining HTML and WebGL effectively and designing responsive layouts, you can deliver immersive 3D experiences to a wide range of users while maintaining user-friendly interfaces. This synergy enhances the overall user engagement and accessibility of your web applications.

7.2. Styling and Positioning with CSS

In this section, we will delve into the importance of styling and positioning when combining WebGL with HTML elements to create visually appealing and interactive 3D graphics. CSS (Cascading Style Sheets) plays a vital role in controlling the presentation and layout of both HTML and WebGL components within a web application.

The Role of CSS in WebGL Integration

CSS is instrumental in defining the visual characteristics of HTML elements and their interaction with WebGL content. Here are key aspects to consider:

1. **Styling HTML Elements**: CSS is used to apply styles such as colors, fonts, and backgrounds to HTML elements that coexist with WebGL. This ensures consistency in the overall design of the web page.
2. **Positioning HTML Elements**: CSS provides precise control over the placement and positioning of HTML elements relative to WebGL canvases or 3D scenes. This control is crucial for creating effective user interfaces.
3. **Responsive Design**: CSS media queries enable responsive design, allowing your WebGL application to adapt to various screen sizes and orientations. This is essential for ensuring a consistent user experience across devices.

Styling HTML Elements

To style HTML elements that are integrated with WebGL, you can use CSS rules. Here's an example of applying styles to an HTML button:

```
<button id="myButton">Click Me</button>

/* CSS to style the button */

#myButton {

background-color: #007acc;

color: white;

padding: 10px 20px;

border: none;

cursor: pointer;

font-size: 16px;

}

#myButton:hover {

background-color: #005c99;

}
```

In this example, we've defined styles for the button, including its background color, text color, padding, and cursor behavior. The :hover pseudo-class changes the button's background color when hovered over.

Positioning HTML Elements

Precise positioning of HTML elements relative to WebGL content can be achieved using CSS positioning properties such as position, top, left, right, and bottom. Here's an example of positioning an HTML div containing a WebGL canvas:

```
<div id="canvasContainer">

<canvas id="webglCanvas"></canvas>

</div>

/* CSS to position the canvas container */

#canvasContainer {

position: relative;

width: 100%;

height: 400px;

}

#webglCanvas {

position: absolute;

top: 0;

left: 0;

width: 100%;

height: 100%;

}
```

In this example, the #canvasContainer div is set to position: relative, which serves as the container for the WebGL canvas. The #webglCanvas element inside it is set to position: absolute, allowing it to occupy the entire container.

Responsive Design

Responsive design ensures that your web application adapts to different screen sizes and orientations. CSS media queries enable you to define styles specific to various breakpoints. For example:

```
/* CSS for larger screens */
@media (min-width: 768px) {
#webglCanvas {
width: 80%;
height: 600px;
}
}
/* CSS for smaller screens */
@media (max-width: 768px) {
#webglCanvas {
width: 100%;
height: 300px;
}
}
```

These media queries adjust the size of the WebGL canvas based on screen width. By applying responsive design principles, you can optimize the layout and presentation of your WebGL content across different devices.

In summary, CSS plays a crucial role in styling, positioning, and ensuring responsive design when integrating WebGL with HTML elements. Leveraging CSS effectively enhances the visual appeal and user experience of your 3D web applications.

7.3. Responsive Design for 3D Graphics

Responsive design is a critical aspect of integrating WebGL content with HTML elements to ensure that your 3D graphics look and function well across a variety of devices, screen sizes, and orientations. In this section, we'll explore responsive design principles specific to 3D graphics and how to adapt your WebGL applications to different viewing contexts.

Why Responsive Design Matters

The proliferation of various devices, from smartphones and tablets to desktop computers and VR headsets, necessitates responsive design for WebGL applications. Here are some reasons why responsive design is crucial:

1. **Cross-Device Compatibility**: Responsive design ensures that your WebGL content is accessible and functional on a wide range of devices, enhancing the reach of your application.
2. **Optimized User Experience**: Adapting to different screen sizes and orientations ensures that users can interact with and view your 3D graphics comfortably, regardless of the

device they are using.
3. **Consistency**: Responsive design maintains a consistent user interface and user experience across platforms, reinforcing your brand identity and user engagement.

CSS Media Queries

CSS media queries are a fundamental tool for responsive design. They allow you to apply different styles based on various conditions, such as screen width, device characteristics, and more. Here's an example of a media query that adjusts the width of a WebGL canvas for different screen sizes:

```
/* CSS for larger screens */

@media (min-width: 768px) {

#webglCanvas {

width: 80%;

height: 600px;

}

}

/* CSS for smaller screens */

@media (max-width: 768px) {

#webglCanvas {

width: 100%;

height: 300px;

}
```

}

In this example, the min-width and max-width conditions target screens with a minimum width of 768 pixels and those with a maximum width of 768 pixels, respectively. Depending on the condition met, the CSS rules apply different dimensions to the WebGL canvas.

Handling Orientation

Responsive design should also consider device orientation, particularly for mobile devices that can be used in both portrait and landscape modes. You can use CSS media queries to adjust styles based on orientation:

```
/* CSS for portrait orientation */

@media (orientation: portrait) {

#webglCanvas {

/* Styles for portrait orientation */

}

}

/* CSS for landscape orientation */

@media (orientation: landscape) {

#webglCanvas {

/* Styles for landscape orientation */

}

}
```

By targeting specific orientations, you can optimize the layout and presentation of your WebGL content to suit the way users hold their devices.

User Interaction on Different Devices

Responsive design should also account for differences in user interaction methods. For example, mobile devices rely on touch controls, while desktop computers use mice and keyboards. You may need to implement touch events, gestures, or alternative navigation methods for mobile users to ensure a seamless experience.

In summary, responsive design for 3D graphics in WebGL involves utilizing CSS media queries to adapt layout and styles, handling device orientation, and considering user interaction methods across various devices. Implementing responsive design principles ensures that your WebGL applications are accessible and enjoyable for a diverse audience.

7.4. Accessibility in WebGL Content

Accessibility is a critical aspect of web development, and it extends to WebGL content as well. Ensuring that your 3D graphics are accessible to all users, including those with disabilities, is both a moral responsibility and, in many regions, a legal requirement. In this section, we'll explore the importance of accessibility in WebGL content and discuss best practices to make your 3D applications inclusive.

The Importance of Accessibility

Accessibility, often abbreviated as "a11y," aims to provide equal access to digital content for people with disabilities. When it comes to WebGL content, accessibility is essential for several reasons:

1. **Inclusivity**: Accessibility ensures that individuals with disabilities can access and interact with your 3D graphics, making your content available to a broader audience.
2. **Legal Compliance**: Many countries have regulations and laws, such as the Americans with Disabilities Act (ADA) in the United States and the Web Content Accessibility Guidelines (WCAG), that mandate accessibility for digital content, including WebGL applications.
3. **Ethical Considerations**: Ensuring accessibility aligns with ethical considerations, demonstrating your commitment to providing equal opportunities for all users.

Best Practices for WebGL Accessibility

Here are some best practices for making your WebGL content more accessible:

1. Semantic HTML Elements:

Use semantic HTML elements where applicable. Properly label and structure your HTML to convey meaning and context to assistive technologies. For example, use <button> for clickable elements and <a> for links.

2. Keyboard Navigation:

Ensure that all interactive elements within your WebGL application can be navigated and activated using a keyboard. Implement keyboard focus management so that users can easily see which element is currently focused.

3. ARIA Roles and Attributes:

Use ARIA (Accessible Rich Internet Applications) roles and attributes to enhance the accessibility of custom WebGL components. ARIA can convey additional information about the roles and states of elements to assistive technologies.

```
<button aria-label="Play" role="button" tabindex="0"
onclick="playVideo()">Play</button>
```

4. Text Alternatives:

Provide text alternatives for non-text content, such as images or 3D models. Use the alt attribute for images and consider providing descriptions for 3D scenes in a way that can be read by screen readers.

5. Color Contrast:

Ensure proper color contrast for text and graphical elements. This is important for users with visual impairments. Tools like WCAG guidelines can help you determine if your color choices meet accessibility standards.

6. Test with Screen Readers:

Regularly test your WebGL content with screen reader software to identify and address accessibility issues. Popular screen readers include JAWS, NVDA, and VoiceOver.

7. Error Handling:

Ensure that error messages and feedback are clear and informative. Users with disabilities should be able to understand and respond to any errors or alerts in your application.

8. Progressive Enhancement:

Follow the principle of progressive enhancement, which means building your WebGL application to work without JavaScript or WebGL enabled. This provides a fallback for users who may have limitations.

9. Documentation and User Guides:

Provide documentation and user guides that explain how to interact with your WebGL content using assistive technologies. Include instructions for keyboard shortcuts, screen reader compatibility, and other accessibility features.

In summary, ensuring accessibility in WebGL content is crucial for providing equal access to all users, complying with legal requirements, and adhering to ethical standards. By following best practices and testing with accessibility tools, you can make your 3D applications more inclusive and user-friendly.

7.5. Dynamic Content Integration

Dynamic content integration in WebGL refers to the process of incorporating interactive and frequently updated content into your 3D graphics. This can enhance user engagement and provide real-time information or functionality within your WebGL application. In this section, we'll explore various ways to integrate dynamic content seamlessly into your WebGL projects.

Types of Dynamic Content

1. **Real-Time Data**: You can integrate real-time data into your WebGL scenes, such as live weather information, stock market updates, or sports scores. This dynamic information can be displayed within the 3D environment or as overlays.
2. **User Interaction**: Allow users to interact with dynamic elements, such as buttons, sliders, or input fields, directly within the WebGL application. These interactions can trigger events, animations, or data updates.
3. **External APIs**: Fetch data from external APIs and display it within your WebGL application. This can include integrating maps, social media feeds, or external databases.
4. **Live Feeds**: Display live video or audio streams within your 3D environment, enhancing the immersive experience. For example, you can integrate a live camera feed from a remote location.

Techniques for Dynamic Content Integration

1. WebGL Libraries:

Utilize WebGL libraries and frameworks that provide built-in support for dynamic content. Some libraries offer components for interactive elements and real-time data visualization, simplifying integration.

2. WebSockets:

Implement WebSockets to establish bidirectional communication between your WebGL application and a server. This enables real-time updates and user interactions without the need for continuous polling.

```
const socket = new WebSocket('wss://example.com');
socket.onmessage = function (event) {
const data = JSON.parse(event.data);
// Update the WebGL scene with the received data
};
```

3. RESTful APIs:

Make HTTP requests to RESTful APIs to retrieve dynamic data. You can use JavaScript libraries like Fetch or Axios to fetch data and update your WebGL application accordingly.

```
fetch('https://api.example.com/data')
.then(response => response.json())
.then(data => {
// Process and display data in WebGL
})
.catch(error => {
console.error('Error fetching data:', error);
```

```
});
```

4. Server-Sent Events (SSE):

Server-Sent Events provide a simple and efficient way to receive updates from a server over a single HTTP connection. It's suitable for applications that require real-time updates.

```
const eventSource = new EventSource('https://example.com/updates');

eventSource.onmessage = function (event) {

const data = JSON.parse(event.data);

// Update the WebGL content based on received events

};
```

5. State Management:

Implement a state management system within your WebGL application to handle dynamic content efficiently. State management libraries like Redux or MobX can help manage complex application states.

6. External Libraries:

Leverage external JavaScript libraries or APIs for specific dynamic content integration needs. For example, you can use the Google Maps API to embed interactive maps within your WebGL scene.

Performance Considerations

While integrating dynamic content can enhance your WebGL application, it's essential to consider performance:

1. **Optimization**: Optimize your code to minimize the impact of dynamic content on performance. Use efficient data structures and algorithms, and avoid unnecessary updates.
2. **Caching**: Implement caching mechanisms for frequently requested data to reduce server load and improve responsiveness.
3. **Throttling and Debouncing**: Control the rate at which dynamic content updates to prevent excessive requests or animations that may overload the user's device.
4. **Fallbacks**: Provide fallbacks for users who may experience issues with dynamic content, such as those with slower internet connections or disabled JavaScript.

By effectively integrating dynamic content into your WebGL projects and addressing performance considerations, you can create engaging and informative 3D experiences that captivate your audience.

8.1. Performance Analysis Tools

Performance is a critical aspect of WebGL development. To create smooth and responsive 3D graphics, it's essential to analyze and optimize the performance of your WebGL applications. In this section, we'll explore various performance analysis tools and techniques that can help you identify bottlenecks and improve your WebGL projects.

Why Performance Analysis Matters

Before diving into specific tools and techniques, let's understand why performance analysis is crucial in WebGL development:

1. **User Experience**: A slow or laggy WebGL application can frustrate users and lead to a poor user experience. Analyzing and optimizing performance can result in smoother interactions and higher user satisfaction.
2. **Compatibility**: Different devices and browsers have varying levels of WebGL support and hardware capabilities. Performance analysis ensures that your application works well across a wide range of configurations.
3. **Efficiency**: Efficient code and resource usage can lead to reduced battery consumption on mobile devices, making your application more energy-efficient.
4. **Scalability**: As your WebGL projects become more complex, performance issues may become more evident. Performance analysis helps you identify areas where optimization is needed to maintain scalability.

Performance Analysis Tools

1. Browser Developer Tools:

Most modern web browsers offer developer tools that include performance analysis features. These tools allow you to profile your WebGL application, monitor frame rates, and identify performance bottlenecks. Google Chrome's DevTools, for example, provides a comprehensive set of performance analysis tools.

2. WebGL Inspector:

WebGL Inspector is a browser extension that specializes in debugging and profiling WebGL applications. It allows you to inspect and modify the state of your WebGL application in real-time, helping you identify issues and optimize performance.

3. GPU Profilers:

GPU profilers, such as NVIDIA Nsight and AMD Radeon GPU Profiler, focus on analyzing the GPU's performance. These tools can help you understand how your WebGL application utilizes the GPU and identify rendering bottlenecks.

4. JavaScript Profilers:

JavaScript profilers, like the one included in browser developer tools, help you analyze the performance of your JavaScript code. You can identify functions that consume significant CPU time and optimize them.

5. Frame Rate Monitors:

Frame rate monitoring tools display real-time frame rates and frame timings, allowing you to detect frame drops and performance spikes.

Monitoring frame rates is crucial for achieving smooth animations and interactions in WebGL.

6. Lighthouse:

Lighthouse is an open-source tool from Google that focuses on web performance and best practices. It not only measures performance but also provides recommendations for improving your WebGL application's speed and efficiency.

Performance Analysis Workflow

Here's a general workflow for using performance analysis tools in WebGL development:

1. **Profile**: Start by profiling your WebGL application using browser developer tools or dedicated tools like WebGL Inspector. Capture performance data during typical interactions.
2. **Analyze**: Examine the collected data to identify performance bottlenecks. Look for functions or operations that consume excessive CPU or GPU resources.
3. **Optimize**: Once you've identified areas that need improvement, work on optimizing your code. This may involve optimizing shaders, reducing unnecessary calculations, or using more efficient algorithms.
4. **Test**: Test the optimized version of your WebGL application to ensure that the changes have a positive impact on performance. Continuously monitor frame rates and other performance metrics.
5. **Iterate**: Performance optimization is an iterative process. Repeat the profiling, analysis, and optimization steps as needed to achieve the desired level of performance.

By incorporating performance analysis tools and following a structured workflow, you can create WebGL applications that deliver a smooth and enjoyable user experience across a variety of devices and browsers.

8.2. Efficient Memory Management

Efficient memory management is a critical aspect of WebGL development. Properly managing memory can help reduce resource consumption, improve application performance, and prevent memory-related issues. In this section, we'll explore memory management techniques and best practices for WebGL.

Why Memory Management Matters

In WebGL, memory is allocated for various resources, including textures, buffers, and shaders. Inefficient memory usage can lead to several problems:

1. **Performance Degradation**: Excessive memory usage can slow down your application, causing frame drops and rendering delays.
2. **Resource Limits**: WebGL has limited GPU memory available. Inefficient memory management can quickly exhaust these resources, leading to rendering failures.
3. **Stability Issues**: Memory leaks or excessive memory consumption can cause your application to crash or become unstable.

Memory Management Techniques

1. Texture Management:

Textures consume a significant amount of GPU memory. To manage textures efficiently:

- Use texture atlases to pack multiple textures into a single texture sheet, reducing memory overhead.
- Implement texture streaming to load and unload textures dynamically based on the camera's view.
- Consider using compressed texture formats like DXT or ETC to reduce memory usage without sacrificing quality.

2. Buffer Management:

Buffer objects, such as vertex and index buffers, are essential for rendering. Efficient buffer management includes:

- Reusing buffers when possible instead of creating new ones.
- Implementing buffer pooling to recycle buffers for objects that share the same attributes.
- Using buffer storage efficiently by avoiding excessive updates.

3. Shader Management:

Shader programs are compiled and linked on the GPU, consuming GPU memory. To manage shaders efficiently:

• Compile and link shaders only when necessary, rather than recompiling them each frame.

• Share shaders across objects with similar rendering requirements.

• Consider using shader permutation techniques to generate optimized shader variants.

4. Garbage Collection:

JavaScript, which is often used in WebGL applications, relies on automatic garbage collection. Avoid creating unnecessary objects and ensure you release WebGL-related resources explicitly when they are no longer needed to prevent memory leaks.

5. Profiling and Monitoring:

Use profiling tools and memory monitors to identify memory usage patterns and potential leaks. Browser developer tools often provide memory profiling features that can help you track memory consumption.

Best Practices

Here are some best practices for efficient memory management in WebGL:

• Create a memory management plan for your application that includes strategies for handling different types of resources.

- Minimize the use of high-resolution textures and complex shaders unless they are essential for your application.
- Implement level-of-detail (LOD) techniques to reduce the quality of objects that are far from the camera's view.
- Monitor memory usage in real-time and set limits to prevent excessive memory consumption.
- Test your application on various devices and browsers to ensure memory efficiency across different platforms.

Efficient memory management is essential for creating WebGL applications that perform well and provide a smooth user experience. By following these techniques and best practices, you can optimize memory usage and avoid common memory-related issues in your WebGL projects.

8.3. Optimizing Render Cycles

Optimizing render cycles is a critical aspect of WebGL development, as it directly impacts the performance of your 3D applications. In this section, we'll explore various techniques and strategies to enhance the efficiency of your render cycles.

Understanding the Render Cycle

The render cycle in WebGL involves several stages, including updating the scene, issuing draw calls, and rendering objects. Here's a high-level overview:

1. **Scene Update**: This stage involves updating object positions, animations, and camera settings.

2. **Culling**: Objects that are not within the camera's view frustum should be culled to avoid unnecessary rendering.
3. **Batching**: Grouping objects with similar rendering properties, such as shaders and materials, can minimize state changes and reduce draw calls.
4. **Rendering**: This stage involves issuing draw calls to render objects, which may include vertex and fragment shader execution.

Techniques for Render Cycle Optimization

1. Frustum Culling:

Implementing frustum culling is essential to avoid rendering objects that are outside the camera's view. This can significantly reduce the number of draw calls and improve performance.

2. Level of Detail (LOD):

Use LOD techniques to reduce the level of detail for objects that are far from the camera. This helps allocate more GPU resources to objects in the foreground, enhancing overall scene quality and performance.

3. Occlusion Culling:

Implement occlusion culling to avoid rendering objects that are occluded by other objects in the scene. Techniques like portal culling and hierarchical occlusion culling can be beneficial.

4. Instancing:

Utilize WebGL's instancing feature to render multiple instances of the same object with a single draw call. This is particularly useful for objects like particles or grass where many identical instances are present.

5. Batch Rendering:

Batch objects with similar rendering properties together to minimize state changes and reduce draw calls. Sorting objects by shader, material, or texture can help achieve this.

6. GPU Optimization:

Optimize your shaders and rendering techniques to make the most of the GPU's capabilities. Minimize the use of costly operations in shaders and use GPU-specific features like texture atlases for efficient texture rendering.

7. Asynchronous Operations:

Consider using asynchronous operations to offload non-essential tasks like texture loading or post-processing to avoid blocking the main render cycle.

8. Frame Budget:

Set a target frame rate and establish a frame budget. Ensure that your rendering operations can complete within the allocated frame time to maintain a smooth and consistent frame rate.

Profiling and Monitoring

Use profiling tools and WebGL debugging extensions to monitor your application's render cycle performance. Profilers can help identify bottlenecks and areas that need optimization.

Best Practices

Here are some best practices to follow when optimizing render cycles in WebGL:

- Profile your application to identify performance bottlenecks and focus your optimization efforts where they matter most.
- Experiment with different techniques and strategies to find the best combination for your specific application.
- Consider implementing a rendering pipeline that allows for efficient sorting and batching of objects.
- Optimize shaders for the target hardware and avoid unnecessary calculations.
- Keep the number of draw calls and state changes to a minimum by grouping similar objects together.

By implementing these techniques and best practices, you can significantly improve the performance of your WebGL applications, ensuring a smooth and responsive 3D experience for users.

8.4. Balancing Quality and Performance

Balancing quality and performance is a crucial aspect of WebGL development. Achieving stunning visual quality while maintaining smooth performance can be challenging. In this section, we'll explore strategies and considerations for striking the right balance between these two factors.

Performance vs. Quality Trade-offs

When developing WebGL applications, you often encounter situations where improving visual quality may negatively impact performance or vice versa. Here are some common trade-offs:

1. **Resolution and Texture Quality**: Using high-resolution textures and detailed models can enhance visual quality but consume more GPU memory and processing power. Consider using lower-resolution textures for distant objects to optimize performance.
2. **Shaders and Effects**: Complex shaders and visual effects can add realism to your scenes but may result in increased GPU load. Evaluate whether certain effects are essential for your application and optimize or simplify them if necessary.
3. **Anti-Aliasing**: Anti-aliasing techniques like MSAA (Multisample Anti-Aliasing) can improve the smoothness of edges but may impact performance. Choose an anti-aliasing level that balances visual quality and performance based on your target hardware.
4. **Shadow Quality**: High-quality shadows with soft edges and realistic penumbra require more rendering passes and can be resource-intensive. Adjust shadow quality settings based on performance constraints.

LOD (Level of Detail)

Implementing Level of Detail (LOD) techniques allows you to dynamically adjust the detail of objects based on their distance from the camera. This helps optimize performance while maintaining visual quality. LOD can be applied to 3D models, textures, and even shaders.

For 3D models, you can switch between different versions of an object with varying levels of detail. Use lower-polygon models for distant objects and higher-polygon models for closer ones.

For textures, create a set of textures with different resolutions. Swap textures based on the object's distance from the camera, using lower-resolution textures for objects that are farther away.

In shaders, simplify calculations or reduce the number of samples for distant pixels to save processing power. This can be particularly effective for post-processing effects like bloom or depth of field.

Dynamic Quality Adjustments

Consider providing users with options to adjust visual quality settings in your WebGL applications. This allows users to tailor the experience to their hardware capabilities and preferences. Common quality settings include texture resolution, shader complexity, and anti-aliasing level.

Profiling and Optimization

Regularly profile your WebGL application to identify performance bottlenecks and areas where quality can be improved. Profilers can help you pinpoint which aspects of your application are consuming the most resources.

Optimization should be an iterative process. As you profile and optimize, make sure to test your application on various hardware configurations to ensure a consistent experience across different devices.

Best Practices

Here are some best practices for balancing quality and performance in WebGL development:

- Prioritize the most critical visual elements for high-quality treatment and optimize the rest.
- Use LOD techniques to reduce the level of detail for distant objects.
- Provide quality settings that users can adjust based on their hardware capabilities.
- Profile and optimize your application regularly to maintain a balance between quality and performance.
- Test your application on different hardware configurations to ensure compatibility and performance consistency.

Finding the right balance between quality and performance is an ongoing process that requires careful consideration and testing. By implementing these strategies and best practices, you can create WebGL applications that deliver both impressive visual quality and responsive performance.

8.5. Handling Large Scale Graphics

Handling large-scale graphics in WebGL can be challenging, especially when dealing with extensive 3D scenes or massive textures. In this section, we'll explore techniques and considerations for efficiently managing and rendering large-scale graphics in WebGL.

Hierarchical Scene Graphs

One effective way to manage large scenes is by using a hierarchical scene graph. A scene graph is a data structure that represents the objects in your 3D scene and their relationships. By organizing objects hierarchically, you can optimize rendering and improve overall performance.

A common approach is to group objects into nodes, where each node represents a part of the scene. This hierarchical structure allows you to perform culling and visibility checks efficiently. Objects outside the camera's view frustum or those obscured by other objects can be culled, reducing the number of objects sent to the GPU for rendering.

Level of Detail (LOD)

As mentioned in the previous section, Level of Detail (LOD) techniques are crucial for handling large-scale graphics. LOD not only applies to objects but also to the entire scenes. For example, you can simplify the geometry and reduce texture resolutions for distant parts of your scene.

Implementing LOD for scenes involves switching between different versions of the scene or parts of it based on the camera's distance. This helps maintain a balance between visual quality and performance, especially when dealing with extensive landscapes or environments.

Texture Atlases and Streaming

Texture atlases are a common optimization technique for managing large textures. Instead of loading individual textures for each object, you can combine multiple textures into a single atlas. This reduces the number of texture switches and minimizes memory usage.

When dealing with extremely large textures, streaming can be helpful. Rather than loading the entire texture upfront, you can load smaller portions of it progressively as needed. This is particularly useful for open-world games or applications with vast environments.

Occlusion Culling

Occlusion culling is a technique that prevents the rendering of objects that are entirely hidden by other objects. It's essential for optimizing scenes with complex geometry. WebGL libraries and frameworks often provide built-in occlusion culling features to help manage large-scale scenes more efficiently.

Asynchronous Loading and Resource Management

When dealing with large-scale graphics, asynchronous loading of assets becomes crucial. Load textures, 3D models, and other resources in the background while your application remains responsive. Use resource management techniques to track the status of loaded assets and ensure they are available when needed.

Chunking and Grid Systems

For applications with vast terrains or environments, consider dividing the world into smaller chunks or using grid systems. Each chunk or grid cell can be loaded and unloaded dynamically based on the camera's position. This approach reduces the amount of data loaded into memory and allows for efficient rendering of large-scale scenes.

Efficient Data Formats

Choose efficient data formats for your 3D models and textures. Consider using compressed texture formats and optimized mesh formats to reduce memory usage and improve loading times.

Profiling and Optimization

Regularly profile your WebGL application to identify performance bottlenecks related to large-scale graphics. Profilers can help you pinpoint areas that require optimization, such as inefficient resource loading or rendering operations.

By applying these techniques and considerations, you can effectively handle large-scale graphics in your WebGL applications. Whether you're creating expansive virtual worlds or dealing with massive datasets, optimizing for performance and memory usage is essential for delivering a smooth user experience.

Chapter 9: Mobile WebGL

9.1. Adapting WebGL for Mobile Devices

Mobile devices have become an integral part of our daily lives, and adapting WebGL applications for these platforms is crucial to reaching a wider audience. In this section, we will explore the challenges and strategies involved in optimizing WebGL content for mobile devices.

Mobile Graphics Capabilities

Before diving into mobile optimization, it's essential to understand the graphics capabilities of different mobile devices. Mobile GPUs vary in performance, supporting different WebGL feature levels. To ensure compatibility, consider testing your WebGL application on a range of devices, from low-end smartphones to high-end tablets.

Responsive Design

One of the first steps in mobile optimization is creating a responsive design for your WebGL application. Responsive design ensures that your content adapts to different screen sizes and orientations. Use CSS media queries to adjust the layout and styling based on the device's characteristics.

Touch and Gesture Controls

Mobile devices rely on touch and gesture controls rather than traditional mouse and keyboard inputs. Implement touch controls that allow users to interact with your WebGL content seamlessly. This may include touch gestures like pinch-to-zoom, swipe, and multi-touch support.

Performance Considerations

Mobile devices often have limited processing power and memory compared to desktop computers. To optimize performance:

- Minimize the number of draw calls and reduce the complexity of 3D scenes.

- Optimize shaders and reduce texture sizes to conserve memory.

- Implement Level of Detail (LOD) techniques to maintain performance on lower-end devices.

- Use requestAnimationFrame for efficient rendering loops.

- Consider using hardware acceleration and web workers for parallel processing.

Mobile Shader Optimization

Shaders play a significant role in WebGL applications, and optimizing shaders for mobile devices is essential. Mobile GPUs may have limitations, so avoid complex and computationally intensive shader operations. Profile and test your shaders on mobile devices to ensure they run smoothly.

Cross-Platform Development Strategies

To target multiple mobile platforms, consider using cross-platform development frameworks and libraries. Three.js, Babylon.js, and Unity WebGL are examples of tools that allow you to create WebGL content that runs on various devices, including mobile.

Handling Screen Resolutions

Mobile devices have a wide range of screen resolutions and pixel densities. Implement techniques like device pixel ratio detection and scaling to ensure your WebGL content looks sharp and consistent on different screens.

Battery Life Optimization

Mobile devices are power-constrained, so optimizing for battery life is crucial. Minimize CPU and GPU usage when the application is in the background or not actively used. Consider implementing features like automatic pausing and resource management to conserve battery.

Testing and Debugging

Testing on real mobile devices is essential for identifying performance bottlenecks and ensuring a smooth user experience. Use browser developer tools and remote debugging tools to analyze and optimize your WebGL application on mobile platforms.

User Experience

Lastly, prioritize the user experience on mobile. Design intuitive touch controls, provide clear instructions, and offer a seamless transition between desktop and mobile versions of your WebGL application.

By following these strategies and best practices, you can adapt your WebGL content for mobile devices, providing a compelling and optimized experience for users on smartphones and tablets.

9.2. Handling Touch and Gesture Controls

Mobile devices rely heavily on touch and gesture controls for user interaction. Implementing these controls effectively in your WebGL applications can significantly enhance the user experience. In this section, we will explore how to handle touch and gesture controls in WebGL.

Touch Event Handling

To capture touch events in WebGL, you can use the Touch Events API provided by web browsers. This API allows you to detect touch interactions, including touchstart, touchmove, and touchend events. Here's an example of how to handle touch events in JavaScript:

```
// Get a reference to your WebGL canvas element

const canvas = document.getElementById('webgl-canvas');

// Add touch event listeners

canvas.addEventListener('touchstart', handleTouchStart, false);

canvas.addEventListener('touchmove', handleTouchMove, false);

canvas.addEventListener('touchend', handleTouchEnd, false);

// Handle touchstart event

function handleTouchStart(event) {

// Retrieve touch positions from the event

const touch = event.touches[0];

const x = touch.clientX;

const y = touch.clientY;
```

```
// Perform actions based on touch coordinates

// Example: Perform a raycast for object selection

}

// Handle touchmove event

function handleTouchMove(event) {

// Handle touch movements, e.g., rotating a 3D object

}

// Handle touchend event

function handleTouchEnd(event) {

// Handle touch release, e.g., stop object rotation

}
```

Gestures and Gesture Libraries

Gestures like pinch-to-zoom, swipe, and multi-finger gestures are common on mobile devices. Implementing these gestures from scratch can be complex. Fortunately, there are JavaScript libraries and frameworks available, such as Hammer.js and ZingTouch, that simplify gesture recognition.

Here's a basic example of how to use Hammer.js for pinch-to-zoom:

```
const canvas = document.getElementById('webgl-canvas');

const mc = new Hammer.Manager(canvas);

// Enable pinch and pan gestures

mc.add(new Hammer.Pinch());
```

```
mc.add(new Hammer.Pan());
// Handle pinch-to-zoom and pan gestures
mc.on('pinch', function (e) {
// Scale your WebGL scene based on the pinch gesture
});
mc.on('pan', function (e) {
// Translate or rotate your WebGL scene based on the pan gesture
});
```

Multi-Touch Support

Mobile devices support multi-touch, allowing users to interact with multiple fingers simultaneously. You can leverage this feature to create more immersive experiences. For example, you can implement two-finger gestures for rotating 3D objects or using three fingers for advanced controls.

Responsiveness and User Feedback

When implementing touch and gesture controls, ensure that your WebGL application is responsive to various touch inputs. Provide visual feedback, such as highlighting interactive elements or displaying gesture instructions, to guide users on how to interact with your content effectively.

By incorporating touch and gesture controls into your WebGL applications, you can make them more accessible and engaging for mobile users, enhancing the overall user experience.

9.3. Performance Considerations on Mobile

Mobile devices come with a diverse range of hardware capabilities, screen sizes, and processing power. Ensuring good performance on mobile WebGL applications is essential for delivering a smooth and enjoyable user experience. In this section, we'll explore various performance considerations when developing for mobile.

1. Device Compatibility Testing

Before deploying your WebGL application to mobile devices, thoroughly test it on different devices and browsers. Mobile fragmentation can lead to varying levels of compatibility and performance. Use emulators and real devices to identify potential issues and optimize accordingly.

2. Resolution and Scaling

Mobile devices have a wide range of screen resolutions and pixel densities. Ensure your WebGL application is responsive and adapts to different screen sizes and orientations. Use the viewport meta tag and CSS media queries to control how your content scales on mobile screens.

```
<meta name="viewport" content="width=device-width, initial-scale=1.0">
```

3. Graphics Quality Settings

Adjust graphics quality settings dynamically based on the device's capabilities. Lower-end devices may struggle with high-resolution textures and complex shaders. Implement a system that automatically adjusts graphics settings for optimal performance.

4. Texture Compression

Use texture compression formats like ETC1, ETC2, or ASTC to reduce memory usage and improve loading times on mobile devices. Compressed textures require less memory bandwidth, benefiting both performance and battery life.

5. Minimize Draw Calls

Reducing the number of draw calls is critical for good performance. Use batching techniques to group similar objects into a single draw call. Additionally, implement efficient frustum culling to avoid rendering objects that are not visible on the screen.

6. Mobile-Friendly Shaders

Optimize shaders for mobile GPUs. Mobile devices may have limited shader capabilities compared to desktop GPUs. Avoid complex shaders and consider simplifying them when targeting mobile platforms.

7. WebGL Extensions

Be mindful of WebGL extensions. Not all extensions are supported on mobile browsers, so check compatibility and provide fallbacks or alternative solutions when needed.

8. Memory Management

Mobile devices typically have limited memory resources. Implement efficient memory management to avoid excessive memory usage and potential crashes. Release unused resources and textures when they are no longer needed.

9. Power Efficiency

Consider power efficiency when designing your WebGL application. Mobile devices rely on battery power, so optimizing resource usage can extend battery life. Minimize CPU and GPU usage when the application is in the background.

10. Testing and Profiling

Use profiling tools like Chrome DevTools or remote debugging to identify performance bottlenecks on mobile devices. Address issues such as high CPU usage, excessive draw calls, or GPU overdraw.

By carefully addressing these performance considerations, you can ensure that your WebGL applications perform well on a wide range of mobile devices, delivering a smooth and responsive user experience.

9.4. Mobile Shader Optimization

Shader optimization is crucial for achieving good performance in WebGL applications on mobile devices. Mobile GPUs have limited processing power compared to desktop GPUs, so efficient shader code is essential. In this section, we'll explore techniques for optimizing shaders on mobile platforms.

1. Minimize Instruction Count

Reduce the number of instructions in your shaders. Mobile GPUs have lower instruction throughput, so shorter shaders perform better. Avoid complex calculations that are not necessary for the visual outcome.

```
// Before optimization
```

```
vec4 color = vec4(1.0, 0.5, 0.0, 1.0);
color.rgb *= 0.8;
color.a = 0.7;
// After optimization
vec4 color = vec4(0.8, 0.4, 0.0, 0.7);
```

2. Avoid Dynamic Branching

Minimize branching in your shader code. Dynamic branches (if statements) can be costly on mobile GPUs. Use conditional (ternary) operators where possible, and try to eliminate unnecessary branches.

```
// Before optimization
if (condition) {
color = vec4(1.0, 0.0, 0.0, 1.0);
} else {
color = vec4(0.0, 1.0, 0.0, 1.0);
}
// After optimization
color = condition ? vec4(1.0, 0.0, 0.0, 1.0) : vec4(0.0, 1.0, 0.0, 1.0);
```

3. Use Texture Atlases

Combine multiple textures into a texture atlas to reduce texture lookups. Fewer texture lookups result in better performance. Ensure your UV coordinates are correctly mapped to the atlas.

4. Mipmap Levels

Generate and use mipmaps for textures. Mipmaps are smaller versions of textures and are used for improving texture quality at different distances. They can also help reduce aliasing and improve performance when sampling textures at various levels of detail.

```
// Use mipmaps

vec4 texColor = texture2D(sampler, texCoord, mipLevel);
```

5. Avoid Complex Math Functions

Avoid using expensive math functions like sqrt, pow, or trigonometric functions within shaders. Use approximations or precompute values when possible.

```
// Before optimization

float distance = length(vec3(x, y, z));

// After optimization

float distance = sqrt(x * x + y * y + z * z);
```

6. Reuse Variables

Reuse variables instead of creating unnecessary temporary variables. Minimize the number of variables used in your shaders to reduce register pressure.

```
// Before optimization

vec3 normal = normalize(someVector);

vec3 result = normal * 2.0;

// After optimization
```

vec3 result = normalize(someVector) * 2.0;

7. Compile-time Constants

Use compile-time constants for values that do not change during shader execution. This allows the compiler to optimize the code more effectively.

// Use a constant

const float PI = 3.14159265359;

By applying these shader optimization techniques, you can improve the performance of your WebGL applications on mobile devices, ensuring a smoother and more responsive experience for users.

9.5. Cross-Platform Development Strategies

Cross-platform development in the context of WebGL involves creating applications that can run smoothly across various web browsers and devices, including desktops, smartphones, and tablets. This section explores key strategies and considerations for achieving cross-platform compatibility in WebGL development.

1. Browser Compatibility

One of the first challenges in cross-platform development is ensuring compatibility with different web browsers. WebGL support can vary among browsers, so it's essential to test your application on multiple browsers, including Chrome, Firefox, Safari, and Edge. Use feature detection to check for WebGL support and provide fallback content for unsupported browsers.

// Check for WebGL support

```
if (typeof WebGLRenderingContext === 'undefined') {
// Provide a fallback or error message
console.error('WebGL is not supported in this browser.');
}
```

2. Mobile Optimization

Mobile devices have unique characteristics, such as smaller screens and touch input, that require specific optimizations. Consider responsive design techniques to adapt your WebGL application's layout and user interface for mobile devices. Implement touch controls and gestures to enhance the mobile user experience.

3. Performance Profiling

Cross-platform development often involves targeting devices with varying performance capabilities. Use performance profiling tools to identify bottlenecks and optimize your application accordingly. Tools like the Chrome DevTools Performance panel and WebGL Analyzer can help you analyze and improve performance.

4. Resolution Independence

Design your WebGL application to be resolution-independent. Use vector graphics or scalable textures to ensure your content looks good on screens with different resolutions and aspect ratios. Avoid hardcoding pixel values for layout and use relative units like percentages.

5. Input Handling

Handle user input in a way that works well across different devices. Support both mouse and touch input for interactions. Use libraries like PointerEvents to simplify input handling for various input methods.

6. Testing on Real Devices

Testing on real devices is crucial for ensuring cross-platform compatibility. Test your WebGL application on a range of devices, including smartphones, tablets, and different desktop configurations. Pay attention to performance, usability, and any device-specific issues.

7. Progressive Enhancement

Follow the principle of progressive enhancement by delivering a basic WebGL experience to all users and enhancing it for more capable devices and browsers. This approach ensures that your application remains accessible to a broader audience.

8. WebGL Frameworks and Libraries

Consider using WebGL frameworks and libraries that offer cross-platform support. Frameworks like Three.js and Babylon.js abstract WebGL complexity and provide compatibility with various browsers and devices out of the box.

9. Version Control and Collaboration

When working on cross-platform projects, version control and collaboration are essential. Use tools like Git and platforms like GitHub or GitLab to manage your codebase, track changes, and collaborate with team members effectively.

10. Documentation and User Guidance

Provide clear documentation and user guidance within your WebGL application. Include instructions for users who may encounter issues or need assistance with specific devices or browsers. Consider creating a support or FAQ section.

By following these cross-platform development strategies, you can ensure that your WebGL applications are accessible and perform well across a wide range of devices and web browsers, delivering a consistent and enjoyable user experience.

Chapter 10: 3D Graphics in Virtual Reality

10.1. Introduction to WebVR

WebVR, short for Web Virtual Reality, is a technology that enables immersive virtual reality experiences directly within web browsers. It allows users to explore virtual environments, interact with 3D content, and experience VR without the need for dedicated VR headsets or software installations. In this section, we will introduce you to the world of WebVR and how it can be leveraged to create engaging 3D graphics experiences on the web.

What is WebVR?

WebVR is an open standard that extends the capabilities of web browsers to provide VR experiences. It is supported by major browsers like Mozilla Firefox and Google Chrome, making it accessible to a broad audience. WebVR allows you to use VR headsets, such as Oculus Rift or HTC Vive, to interact with 3D content hosted on websites. Additionally, it can work with smartphone-based VR solutions like Google Cardboard.

WebVR Features and Benefits

WebVR offers several features and benefits that make it a compelling choice for developers:

- **Cross-Platform Compatibility:** WebVR is designed to work across different devices and platforms, making it accessible to a wide range of users.

• **No Installation Required:** Users can access WebVR experiences directly from their web browsers, eliminating the need for additional software installations.

• **Wide Accessibility:** Since WebVR can run on smartphones, desktops, and VR headsets, it has the potential to reach a large and diverse audience.

• **Interactive 3D Content:** WebVR enables the creation of interactive 3D content, immersive environments, and VR applications that can engage users in new and exciting ways.

Getting Started with WebVR

To get started with WebVR development, you'll need the following:

1. **WebVR-Enabled Browser:** Make sure you are using a browser that supports WebVR, such as Mozilla Firefox or Google Chrome.
2. **VR Headset (Optional):** While WebVR can be experienced without a headset, having one can provide a more immersive experience. Popular options include Oculus Rift, HTC Vive, or even smartphone-based solutions like Google Cardboard.
3. **WebVR Framework or Library:** Consider using a WebVR framework or library like A-Frame or Three.js, which simplifies the creation of WebVR content.
4. **3D Content:** You'll need 3D models, scenes, or environments to create your WebVR experience. These can be created using 3D modeling software or obtained from online libraries.

Creating WebVR Content

WebVR content is typically created using a combination of HTML, JavaScript, and 3D assets. Here's a simple example of a WebVR scene using A-Frame:

```
<!DOCTYPE html>

<html>

<head>

<meta name="viewport" content="width=device-width, initial-scale=1.0">

<script src="https://aframe.io/releases/1.2.0/aframe.min.js"></script>

</head>

<body>

<a-scene vr-mode-ui="enabled: false">

<a-box position="0 1 -3" rotation="0 45 0" color="#4CC3D9"></a-box>

<a-sphere position="0 1.25 -5" radius="1.25" color="#EF2D5E"></a-sphere>

<a-cylinder position="0 0.75 -3" radius="0.5" height="1.5" color="#FFC65D"></a-cylinder>

<a-plane position="0 0 -4" rotation="-90 0 0" width="4" height="4" color="#7BC8A4"></a-plane>

</a-scene>
```

</body>

</html>

This example creates a simple WebVR scene with geometric shapes using A-Frame. Users with VR headsets can explore this scene in virtual reality directly from their browsers.

WebVR and Beyond

WebVR is just the beginning of web-based virtual reality experiences. With the advent of WebXR (Web Extended Reality), the capabilities of web-based VR and AR (Augmented Reality) are expanding. Developers can create mixed reality experiences that blend the physical and digital worlds. In the next sections, we will explore how to create WebVR and WebXR experiences, including interactive 3D scenes and user interactions.

10.2. Creating Your First VR Scene in WebGL

In this section, we will dive into the practical aspects of creating your first virtual reality (VR) scene using WebGL. We'll explore the essential components and code snippets to get you started on the exciting journey of building VR experiences for the web.

Setting Up Your Development Environment

Before you start creating VR scenes, ensure that you have a suitable development environment. Here are the initial steps:

1. **WebGL Knowledge:** Familiarize yourself with WebGL, as it forms the foundation for creating VR content on the web.

2. **Text Editor or IDE:** Use a code editor or integrated development environment (IDE) of your choice. Popular options include Visual Studio Code, Sublime Text, or WebStorm.
3. **Local Web Server:** To avoid cross-origin issues, consider running a local web server. You can use tools like Node.js with Express or Python's SimpleHTTPServer for this purpose.

Creating a Basic VR Scene

Let's start by creating a basic VR scene using WebGL. Here's a simplified example:

```
<!DOCTYPE html>

<html lang="en">

<head>

<meta charset="UTF-8">

<title>My First VR Scene</title>

</head>

<body>

<canvas id="vr-canvas"></canvas>

<script>

const canvas = document.getElementById('vr-canvas');

const gl = canvas.getContext('webgl');

// Define vertex and fragment shaders here
```

```
// Set up your 3D scene, shaders, and other components

function render() {

// Implement rendering logic here

// Use requestAnimationFrame for smooth animations

requestAnimationFrame(render);

}

render(); // Start rendering loop

</script>

</body>

</html>
```

In this HTML template, we have an empty <canvas> element where our VR scene will be displayed. We also include a JavaScript section for WebGL setup and rendering. Here are the steps to proceed:

1. **Define Shaders:** Create vertex and fragment shaders to control the appearance and behavior of your VR scene. Shaders are essential for WebGL rendering and allow you to manipulate vertices and pixels.
2. **Set Up the 3D Scene:** Initialize your 3D scene, including camera settings, lighting, and any 3D objects you want to display in the VR environment.
3. **Rendering Loop:** Implement a rendering loop using requestAnimationFrame. This loop continuously updates and redraws your VR scene to provide a smooth and responsive experience.
4. **Interactivity (Optional):** Depending on your VR

application, you may want to add interactivity using JavaScript. This can include user input, animations, and interactions within the VR environment.

Testing Your VR Scene

To test your VR scene, save the HTML file and open it in a WebGL-enabled web browser. You should see a blank canvas, which is the starting point for building your VR content. Debugging and further development can be done using browser developer tools.

Next Steps

Creating a VR scene is just the beginning. To build more immersive and interactive VR experiences, you can explore libraries and frameworks like A-Frame or Three.js, which simplify VR development and offer extensive features. Additionally, you can integrate VR headset compatibility for a truly immersive experience.

In the next sections, we will delve deeper into VR development, including user interactions, performance optimization, and creating engaging VR content.

10.3. Interactivity in Virtual Reality

Interactivity is a crucial aspect of creating engaging and immersive virtual reality (VR) experiences. In this section, we will explore various techniques and considerations for implementing interactivity in your VR scenes using WebGL.

User Input in VR

VR experiences often rely on user input to allow users to interact with the virtual environment. There are several ways to capture user input in VR:

1. **Head Tracking:** VR headsets typically include sensors that track the user's head movement. You can use this data to update the user's view in the VR scene, creating a sense of presence.
2. **Controller Input:** Many VR systems come with hand controllers or motion controllers. These controllers can be used to capture hand gestures, trigger actions, and interact with objects in the virtual world.
3. **Voice Commands:** Some VR applications support voice recognition, allowing users to control the environment by speaking commands.
4. **Gaze-Based Interaction:** Gaze-based interaction involves tracking where the user is looking. It can be used for selecting objects or triggering actions by simply looking at them.

Implementing Interactivity

To implement interactivity in your VR scene, you'll need to integrate user input with your WebGL application. Here are some steps to get you started:

1. **Capture Input Data:** Depending on the input method you choose (head tracking, controllers, etc.), you'll need to capture data from the VR hardware. Most VR platforms provide SDKs or APIs for this purpose.
2. **Handle Input Events:** In your JavaScript code, create event handlers to respond to user input. For example, if

you're using hand controllers, you might have event listeners for button presses or gestures.

3. **Update the Scene:** When user input is detected, update the VR scene accordingly. This could involve moving or rotating objects, triggering animations, or changing the environment based on user actions.
4. **Feedback:** Provide feedback to the user to confirm that their input has been recognized. This can include visual cues, sound effects, or haptic feedback (vibrations) depending on the VR hardware.

Example: Interactive VR Menu

Let's consider a simple example of an interactive VR menu. In this scenario, the user can point at menu items with a controller and select them:

```
// Example event handler for controller input

controller.addEventListener('buttonpress', (event) => {

const selectedObject = detectIntersection(controller.ray, menuItems);

if (selectedObject) {

// Perform the action associated with the selected menu item

selectedObject.onClick();

}

});
```

In this code snippet:

- We have a controller event listener that responds to button presses.

- We use a ray casting technique to detect which menu item the controller is pointing at.

- When a menu item is selected, we execute the associated action, such as navigating to a different part of the VR experience.

Optimizing for Performance

When implementing interactivity in VR, it's essential to consider performance. VR applications require consistent high frame rates to prevent motion sickness and provide a smooth experience. To achieve this, optimize your code, minimize rendering complexity, and use efficient algorithms for interactions.

Conclusion

Interactivity is a fundamental component of creating compelling VR experiences in WebGL. Whether you're building a VR game, educational simulation, or virtual tour, thoughtful implementation of user input and interactions can greatly enhance the immersion and engagement of your VR content. As you delve deeper into VR development, explore advanced techniques, such as physics simulations, teleportation, and hand tracking, to create innovative and enjoyable VR experiences.

10.4. Performance Tuning for VR

Achieving optimal performance is critical when developing virtual reality (VR) experiences with WebGL. VR applications demand consistent high frame rates and low latency to ensure a comfortable and immersive experience for users. In this section, we'll explore performance tuning techniques specific to VR development in WebGL.

Frame Rate and Motion Sickness

Maintaining a stable frame rate, typically 90 frames per second (FPS) or higher, is essential in VR to prevent motion sickness. When frame rates drop or vary significantly, users can experience discomfort and nausea. Therefore, performance optimization is crucial to deliver a smooth and enjoyable VR experience.

Optimizing Render Pipeline

Here are some performance tuning tips for your VR WebGL applications:

1. **Level of Detail (LOD):** Implement LOD techniques to render high-detail models when they are close to the user and switch to lower-detail models for distant objects. This reduces the GPU load.
2. **Culling:** Implement frustum culling and occlusion culling to prevent rendering objects that are outside the user's field of view or hidden by other objects.
3. **Texture Compression:** Use texture compression formats like WebP, KTX, or Basis Universal to reduce memory usage and improve loading times.
4. **Shader Optimization:** Profile and optimize your shaders for performance. Consider reducing the number of shader passes and minimizing texture lookups.
5. **Batching:** Combine objects with similar materials and shaders into batches to reduce draw calls and improve rendering efficiency.

6. **Geometry Instancing:** Use GPU instancing to render multiple instances of the same object with a single draw call, reducing CPU overhead.
7. **GPU-Based Physics:** Implement physics simulations using GPU-based techniques like WebGPU or WebGL 2.0 to offload physics calculations from the CPU.

Minimizing Latency

Reducing latency is another critical aspect of VR performance:

1. **Input Latency:** Minimize input-to-photon latency by optimizing the input handling pipeline. Ensure that user actions have an immediate impact in the VR environment.
2. **Prediction and Asynchronous Timewarp:** Implement prediction algorithms and asynchronous timewarp techniques to compensate for missed frames and reduce perceived motion-to-photon latency.
3. **Buffering and Preloading:** Buffer and preload assets to reduce loading times during VR experiences. This includes 3D models, textures, and audio files.

Testing and Profiling

Regularly test your VR application on different VR headsets and hardware configurations to ensure it performs well across various devices. Use profiling tools and performance monitoring to identify bottlenecks and optimize specific parts of your code.

Simplifying Geometry

Simplify complex 3D models to reduce the polygon count and vertex shader load. Tools like Blender and third-party libraries can help automate this process. Consider using LODs (Level of Detail) to render simpler versions of objects when they are farther away from the user.

Texture Atlas

Create texture atlases by packing multiple textures into a single image. This reduces the number of texture swaps during rendering, improving performance. Use tools or scripts to automate the creation of texture atlases.

Object Pooling

Implement object pooling for frequently used objects in your VR scene. Instead of creating and destroying objects repeatedly, reuse them to reduce memory allocations and CPU overhead.

Caching and Batching

Cache frequently accessed data and batch similar rendering operations together. For example, batch rendering calls for objects that share the same material or shader to minimize draw calls and improve rendering efficiency.

Asynchronous Loading

Load assets asynchronously to prevent blocking the main thread. Use web workers or asynchronous functions to load and initialize assets in the background while the VR experience continues running.

Conclusion

Performance tuning is a continuous process in VR WebGL development. By optimizing your VR application for frame rate, latency, and resource usage, you can ensure that users have a comfortable and immersive experience across a wide range of VR hardware. Regular testing, profiling, and iteration are key to achieving VR performance excellence.

10.5. Future of Web-Based Virtual Reality

The field of web-based virtual reality (WebVR) is evolving rapidly, opening up exciting possibilities for immersive experiences on the web. In this section, we'll explore the future trends and advancements expected in WebVR.

1. WebXR API Adoption

WebXR is an evolving standard that encompasses both virtual reality (VR) and augmented reality (AR). It provides a unified API for accessing XR (Extended Reality) devices, making it easier for developers to create cross-platform VR and AR experiences on the web. As the WebXR API matures, we can expect broader adoption and more feature-rich WebXR experiences.

2. WebAssembly and Performance

WebAssembly (Wasm) is a technology that allows running high-performance, low-level code on web browsers. In the context of WebVR, WebAssembly can enable more complex and efficient VR applications by harnessing the full power of the underlying hardware. Expect to see WebAssembly used extensively for VR content optimization.

3. Progressive Web Apps (PWAs) in VR

Progressive Web Apps (PWAs) are web applications that offer a native app-like experience on the web. In the future, we can anticipate the development of PWAs that seamlessly integrate with

VR headsets, providing users with immersive web experiences accessible directly from their VR devices.

4. Web3D Standards

The development of open standards for 3D graphics and interactivity on the web is ongoing. These standards will allow for richer and more interactive 3D content on websites. Technologies like glTF (the GL Transmission Format) for 3D models and WebGPU for low-level graphics access are paving the way for improved WebVR experiences.

5. VR Social Platforms

Social interaction in virtual reality is a growing trend. Expect to see more VR social platforms where users can meet, socialize, and collaborate in virtual spaces. WebVR will play a significant role in making these experiences accessible directly from web browsers.

6. VR E-Commerce

Virtual reality offers unique opportunities for e-commerce. In the future, we may see VR showrooms and shopping experiences where users can explore products in 3D, try them out virtually, and make purchases—all within the web browser.

7. Education and Training

WebVR has the potential to revolutionize education and training by offering immersive learning experiences. As WebVR technology advances, we can anticipate a wider range of educational content and tools accessible to students and professionals alike.

8. Accessibility and Inclusivity

WebVR developers are increasingly focused on making immersive experiences accessible to all users, including those with disabilities. Expect to see advancements in VR accessibility features and guidelines to ensure inclusivity.

9. User-Generated Content

User-generated content (UGC) is likely to become more prevalent in WebVR. Platforms and tools that enable users to create and share their VR experiences will contribute to a diverse and vibrant ecosystem of VR content.

10. Cross-Platform Compatibility

As the WebVR ecosystem grows, there will be a continued emphasis on cross-platform compatibility. Developers will strive to create VR experiences that work seamlessly across a variety of VR headsets and web browsers.

In conclusion, the future of web-based virtual reality is promising, with ongoing developments in standards, performance, and accessibility. As technology continues to advance, we can look forward to more immersive, interactive, and accessible WebVR experiences that will shape the way we interact with the web. WebVR is poised to become a significant part of the evolving web landscape, offering exciting possibilities for both developers and users.

Chapter 11: Augmented Reality with WebGL

11.1. Fundamentals of Web-based Augmented Reality

Augmented Reality (AR) is a technology that blends digital content with the real world. It overlays computer-generated information, such as images, videos, or 3D models, onto the user's view of the physical environment. In the context of the web, web-based Augmented Reality (WebAR) is becoming increasingly popular due to its accessibility and cross-platform compatibility. This section will introduce you to the fundamentals of WebAR, its applications, and the key concepts you need to understand.

Understanding Augmented Reality

Augmented Reality enhances the real world by adding virtual elements that are perceivable through various devices, such as smartphones, tablets, smart glasses, or web browsers. It differs from Virtual Reality (VR), where the user is fully immersed in a computer-generated environment. AR enriches the real world rather than replacing it entirely.

Key Components of Augmented Reality

1. Marker or Trigger

- In WebAR, a marker or trigger is an object or pattern in the physical world that serves as a reference point for placing digital content. It can be an image, a QR code, a specific object, or even a geolocation.

2. Tracking

- Tracking is the process of continuously monitoring and recognizing the marker's position and orientation in real-time. It ensures that the digital content aligns with the physical world correctly.

3. Rendering

- Rendering involves displaying virtual objects or information onto the user's view. It must match the user's perspective and align with the tracked marker.

WebAR Technologies

WebAR leverages web technologies like HTML, CSS, and JavaScript to create augmented experiences accessible through web browsers. Some popular WebAR technologies and libraries include:

- AR.js
- three.js[4]
- A-Frame[5]

These libraries simplify the development of WebAR applications by providing pre-built components and APIs for marker detection, tracking, and rendering.

Applications of WebAR

WebAR has a wide range of applications, including:

---

4. https://threejs.org/

5. https://aframe.io/

- **Marketing and Advertising:** Brands use WebAR to create interactive and engaging advertising campaigns.

- **Education:** It enhances learning experiences by providing interactive educational content.

- **Gaming:** Games can integrate AR elements into their gameplay, creating more immersive experiences.

- **Navigation:** WebAR can assist users with navigation and location-based services.

In the following sections of this chapter, we'll delve deeper into WebAR development, including the tools and libraries you can use to create your own augmented reality experiences.

11.2. AR Toolkit for WebGL

Augmented Reality (AR) development can be complex, but there are libraries and frameworks that make it more accessible. In this section, we'll explore the AR Toolkit, a powerful open-source library that enables developers to create WebAR experiences with ease.

Introduction to AR Toolkit

AR Toolkit, also known as ARToolKit, is an open-source tracking library for creating augmented reality applications. Originally developed by Hirokazu Kato, it has been widely used for AR development on various platforms, including the web. AR Toolkit is designed to detect and track markers in real-time, making it a valuable tool for building WebAR applications.

Features of AR Toolkit

Marker Detection

AR Toolkit excels in marker detection. It can identify predefined markers from a camera feed, allowing you to overlay digital content on top of them. Markers can be simple black-and-white patterns or more complex images.

Camera Pose Estimation

One of the essential features of AR Toolkit is its ability to estimate the pose (position and orientation) of the camera in real-time. This information is crucial for rendering virtual objects accurately in relation to the real world.

Open Source and Cross-Platform

AR Toolkit is open-source, which means you can modify and customize it to suit your needs. It also supports multiple platforms, including web browsers, making it versatile for WebAR development.

Markerless Tracking

While AR Toolkit is known for marker-based tracking, it also supports markerless tracking, where the system detects and tracks objects without predefined markers. This feature can be especially useful for certain types of WebAR applications.

Using AR Toolkit in WebAR Development

To get started with AR Toolkit in WebAR development, you'll need to include the library in your project. You can find the latest version on the official AR Toolkit website or include it via a Content Delivery Network (CDN). Once you have AR Toolkit integrated into your web application, you can start creating AR experiences by defining markers, setting up tracking, and rendering virtual content.

Here's a simplified example of how to use AR Toolkit in HTML and JavaScript:

```
<!DOCTYPE html>

<html lang="en">

<head>

<meta charset="UTF-8">

<title>WebAR with AR Toolkit</title>

</head>

<body>

<video id="video" autoplay playsinline></video>

<canvas id="canvas" width="640" height="480"></canvas>

<script src="https://cdn.jsdelivr.net/npm/artoolkit"></script>

<script>

// Initialize ARToolkit

const video = document.getElementById('video');
```

```
const canvas = document.getElementById('canvas');

const context = canvas.getContext('2d');

const arController = new ARController(video, 'https://cdn.jsdelivr.net/npm/artoolkit', {

cameraParametersUrl: 'camera_para.dat',

onSuccess: function (arController) {

arController.loadMarker('patt.hiro', function(markerId) {

arController.trackPatternMarkerId(markerId);

});

}

});

// Start the video feed

navigator.mediaDevices.getUserMedia({ video: true }).then(function (stream) {

video.srcObject = stream;

}).catch(function (error) {

console.error('Unable to access the camera: ' + error);

});

</script>

</body>

</html>
```

This example sets up a simple WebAR application using AR Toolkit. It initializes the AR controller, loads a predefined marker ('patt.hiro' in this case), and starts the video feed from the user's camera. When the marker is detected, you can add code to render 3D models or other content on top of it.

AR Toolkit provides various functions and options for more advanced WebAR development, such as handling multiple markers, markerless tracking, and 3D object rendering. By exploring the documentation and examples provided by AR Toolkit, you can create engaging augmented reality experiences for the web.

11.3. Designing Interactive AR Experiences

Designing interactive augmented reality (AR) experiences is a creative process that combines the real world with virtual elements. In this section, we'll explore the key principles and considerations for designing AR experiences that engage users and provide meaningful interactions.

User-Centered Design

User-centered design (UCD) is a fundamental principle when designing interactive AR experiences. It involves understanding your target audience, their needs, and how they will interact with your AR application. Here are some UCD considerations:

User Research: Conduct user research to identify user preferences, expectations, and pain points related to AR. This can involve surveys, interviews, and usability testing.

User Persona: Create user personas to represent your target audience. Understand their demographics, motivations, and

goals.

Contextual Inquiry: Study the context in which users will interact with AR. Consider factors like lighting conditions, physical space, and device capabilities.

User Flow: Design user flows that guide users through the AR experience. Consider how users will initiate interactions and navigate virtual content.

Natural Interactions

AR experiences should strive for natural and intuitive interactions. The goal is to make users feel like they are seamlessly interacting with virtual objects in the real world. Here are some principles to achieve this:

Gesture Recognition: Implement gesture recognition to allow users to interact with AR content using natural hand movements. For example, pinch-to-zoom or swipe gestures can control virtual objects.

Voice Commands: Integrate voice recognition to enable users to interact with AR through voice commands. Users can verbally control actions, such as selecting objects or changing settings.

Touch and Tap: Leverage touch and tap interactions on touch-enabled devices. Users can tap virtual buttons, drag objects, or interact with on-screen UI elements.

Feedback and Guidance

Providing feedback and guidance is crucial in AR experiences. Users should receive clear feedback when they perform actions or interact with virtual objects. Consider these aspects:

Visual Feedback: Use visual cues such as animations, highlights, or tooltips to provide feedback when users interact with AR elements.

Audio Feedback: Incorporate audio cues and sounds to enhance the user experience. For example, a satisfying sound effect can play when an action is successfully completed.

Onboarding: Create an onboarding process that guides users through the AR experience. Teach them how to interact with virtual content and provide instructions when needed.

Real-World Integration

Successful AR experiences seamlessly blend virtual content with the real world. Consider the following principles:

Spatial Awareness: Use environmental data to make virtual objects aware of the physical space. Objects should interact realistically with the environment, such as casting shadows or aligning with surfaces.

Anchoring: Use anchor points or markers to position virtual objects in the real world. Anchors ensure that virtual content remains stable and aligned with the physical environment.

Occlusion: Implement occlusion to make virtual objects appear behind real-world objects when appropriate. This enhances the illusion of integration.

User Testing and Iteration

User testing is a crucial part of designing interactive AR experiences. Conduct usability testing with real users to gather feedback and insights. Iterate on your design based on user feedback to improve usability and engagement.

Example AR Interaction Design

Here's a simplified example of designing an interactive AR experience:

Suppose you're creating an AR museum guide application. Users point their mobile devices at museum exhibits to access additional information. The design considerations would include:

- **Gesture Recognition:** Users can pinch to zoom in on exhibits for detailed information or swipe left or right to navigate between exhibits.

- **Voice Commands:** Users can activate voice commands to ask questions like, "Tell me about the artist" or "Translate this description."

- **Visual Feedback:** Tapping on an exhibit highlights it and displays relevant information. Pinching to zoom provides a magnification effect.

- **Onboarding:** When users first launch the app, they receive a brief tutorial on how to interact with exhibits.

- **Spatial Awareness:** Virtual exhibit labels align with the physical exhibits, and virtual tour guides appear as if they are standing near the user.

Designing interactive AR experiences requires creativity, empathy for users, and a deep understanding of AR technology. By following user-centered design principles and considering natural interactions, feedback, real-world integration, and user testing, you can create compelling and engaging AR applications that captivate your audience.

11.4. Integration with Real-World Data

Augmented reality (AR) experiences often benefit from integrating real-world data to provide users with contextually relevant information. This section explores how to incorporate various types of real-world data into AR applications, enhancing the user experience and delivering valuable insights.

Geolocation Data

Integrating geolocation data is a powerful way to make AR experiences location-aware. Here are some ways to incorporate geolocation data into your AR application:

GPS Integration: Utilize the device's GPS capabilities to determine the user's precise location. This can be used to overlay AR content specific to their surroundings, such as pointing out nearby points of interest.

Geofencing: Implement geofencing to trigger AR content or notifications when a user enters or exits a predefined geographic area. For example, an AR app can provide information about historical landmarks when users approach them.

Maps Integration: Combine AR with mapping services like Google Maps to display real-time directions, nearby businesses, or points of interest within the AR view.

Object Recognition

Object recognition technology enables AR applications to identify and interact with physical objects in the real world. Here are some ways to incorporate object recognition:

***Image Recognition:** Use image recognition to identify specific objects, images, or symbols. For instance, scanning a logo or artwork can trigger related AR content or information.*

***Barcode and QR Code Scanning:** Enable AR apps to scan barcodes and QR codes on products or items. This can provide users with product details, pricing, or links to online resources.*

***Marker-Based Tracking:** Implement marker-based tracking, where predefined markers placed in the real world are recognized by the AR app. These markers can trigger 3D models, animations, or information overlays.*

Environmental Sensors

Leveraging environmental sensors in AR applications enhances the perception of the physical world. Here are some ways to integrate environmental sensor data:

Light and Ambient Sensors: Adjust the brightness and appearance of AR content based on ambient light conditions. This ensures that virtual objects appear natural within their environment.

Proximity Sensors: Utilize proximity sensors to detect how close a user is to an object or surface. AR apps can respond by providing more detailed information or resizing virtual content.

Gyroscopes and Accelerometers: Incorporate data from gyroscopes and accelerometers to create immersive AR experiences. For example, users can interact with virtual objects by tilting or moving their devices.

Real-Time Data Feeds

Integrating real-time data feeds is essential for delivering up-to-date information in AR applications. Here are some examples of real-time data integration:

Social Media Feeds: Display live social media updates, such as tweets or posts related to the user's location or interests, within the AR view.

Weather Data: Overlay real-time weather data onto the AR scene, providing users with current weather conditions and forecasts for their location.

Traffic and Transportation Information: Integrate traffic and public transportation data to help users plan their routes and avoid congested areas.

User-Generated Content

Allowing users to contribute content to AR experiences can foster community engagement and enrich the application. Consider these options:

User Reviews and Ratings: Enable users to leave reviews or ratings for AR-related points of interest. This user-generated content can help others make informed decisions.

Photo Sharing: Allow users to capture and share AR experiences with their photos and comments, creating a dynamic and user-driven ecosystem.

User-Generated AR Content: Empower users to create their AR content or augment existing experiences. This can lead to a diverse range of user-generated AR interactions.

Data Privacy and Permissions

When integrating real-world data into AR applications, it's crucial to respect user privacy and adhere to data protection regulations. Always request explicit user consent before accessing sensitive data like location or personal information. Provide clear and transparent privacy policies to build trust with your users.

Example: Real-World Data Integration

Imagine developing an AR navigation app for travelers. Here's how you could integrate various types of real-world data:

- **Geolocation Data:** Use GPS to pinpoint the user's location and show nearby points of interest. Geofencing could trigger AR notifications for attractions or restaurants when the user enters specific areas.

- **Object Recognition:** Implement image recognition to identify landmarks, historical sites, or famous artworks. Scanning QR codes at restaurants could provide menus and reviews.

- **Environmental Sensors:** Adjust the app's appearance based on ambient light conditions, ensuring readability in various lighting environments.

- **Real-Time Data Feeds:** Include real-time weather updates and traffic information within the AR view, helping travelers plan their activities.

- **User-Generated Content:** Let users leave reviews, tips, and photos for places they visit, creating a community of travelers sharing their experiences.

Integrating real-world data enhances the functionality and relevance of AR applications. By combining geolocation, object recognition, environmental sensors, real-time data feeds, and user-generated content, you can create immersive AR experiences that provide valuable information in context. However, always prioritize user privacy and data protection when working with real-world data in AR applications.

11.5. Case Studies in WebGL AR

In this section, we'll explore several case studies that demonstrate the practical applications of WebGL in augmented reality (AR). These real-world examples showcase the versatility and potential of combining WebGL and AR technologies to create immersive and interactive experiences.

Case Study 1: AR Product Visualization

Scenario: A furniture retailer wants to enhance its online shopping experience by allowing customers to visualize how their products would look in their homes before making a purchase.

Solution: The retailer develops an AR application that uses WebGL to render 3D models of furniture items in real-time. Customers can use their smartphones or tablets to view their space through the device's camera and place virtual furniture within it. They can rotate, resize, and move the virtual furniture to find the perfect fit. WebGL ensures smooth and realistic rendering of 3D models, and AR markers on the floor help anchor the virtual objects accurately.

Benefits: This AR solution increases customer engagement and confidence, leading to higher conversion rates. Shoppers can make informed decisions about furniture purchases, reducing returns and improving overall satisfaction.

Case Study 2: Educational AR Biology App

Scenario: A biology teacher wants to create an engaging learning experience for students by bringing biology concepts to life through AR.

Solution: The teacher develops an AR app using WebGL to render 3D models of biological structures such as cells, organs, and organisms. Students can use their mobile devices to explore these 3D models in AR. WebGL ensures that the models are detailed and visually accurate. The app also includes interactive elements like labels, quizzes, and animations to reinforce learning.

Benefits: The educational AR app enhances students' understanding of biology by providing a hands-on and immersive learning experience. Complex biological structures become accessible and easier to comprehend, leading to improved learning outcomes.

Case Study 3: AR Navigation for Museums

Scenario: A museum wants to offer visitors an interactive and informative way to navigate through its exhibits.

Solution: The museum develops an AR navigation app that uses WebGL to create a virtual guide. Visitors can point their smartphones at exhibits, and the app recognizes markers associated with each exhibit. It overlays relevant information, historical context, and multimedia content onto the visitor's screen. WebGL ensures that 3D models and animations of historical artifacts are displayed accurately and with high visual fidelity.

Benefits: The AR navigation app enhances the museum experience, making it more engaging and educational. Visitors gain a deeper understanding of the exhibits and their historical significance, leading to increased visitor satisfaction and a desire to return.

Case Study 4: AR Maintenance and Repair Assistance

Scenario: A manufacturing company wants to improve the efficiency of its maintenance and repair processes for complex machinery.

Solution: The company develops an AR maintenance app that uses WebGL to render 3D models of machinery components. Maintenance technicians wear AR glasses equipped with cameras. When they look at a machine, the app recognizes it and overlays interactive 3D models of the machine's internals, highlighting components that require maintenance or repair. WebGL ensures that the 3D models are realistic and responsive.

Benefits: The AR maintenance app streamlines maintenance processes, reduces downtime, and minimizes errors. Technicians can quickly identify and address issues, resulting in cost savings and increased machinery uptime.

Case Study 5: AR Tourism and Historical Exploration

Scenario: A city wants to attract tourists by offering an immersive way to explore its historical sites and landmarks.

Solution: The city develops an AR tourism app using WebGL to create 3D reconstructions of historical sites. Tourists can use their smartphones or AR glasses to view these reconstructions overlaid onto the real-world locations. WebGL ensures that the historical reconstructions are visually appealing and accurate. The app also provides historical information, audio guides, and interactive quizzes.

Benefits: The AR tourism app enhances the tourist experience by making historical sites come to life. Visitors gain a deeper appreciation for the city's history, and tourism revenues increase.

These case studies illustrate how WebGL can be a valuable component in AR applications across various industries, from retail and education to museums, manufacturing, and tourism. WebGL's ability to render realistic 3D models and provide interactive experiences contributes to the success of these AR solutions, resulting in improved user engagement, learning outcomes, and operational efficiency.

Chapter 12: Creative Coding and Art

12.1. Expressive Graphics with WebGL

In this section, we will explore the world of creative coding and artistic expression using WebGL. Creative coding is a practice that combines programming and art to create interactive and visually stunning digital experiences. WebGL, with its ability to render complex 3D graphics in real-time, is a powerful tool for artists and developers alike to push the boundaries of creative expression.

The Intersection of Code and Art

Creative coding blurs the lines between programming and artistry. It allows artists and developers to harness the computational power of computers to generate art, animations, and interactive experiences. WebGL provides a canvas for this creativity by enabling the creation of dynamic, real-time 3D graphics directly in web browsers. Whether you're an artist looking to experiment with new mediums or a developer interested in exploring the artistic side of programming, WebGL offers a rich playground.

Building Interactive Art

With WebGL, you can build interactive art pieces that respond to user input, creating a unique and engaging experience. By combining JavaScript with WebGL, you can capture user interactions like mouse movements, clicks, or keyboard inputs to influence the visuals or behaviors of your creations. This interactivity can turn a static artwork into a dynamic and engaging piece that users can explore and interact with.

Shaders for Artistic Expression

One of the most powerful aspects of WebGL for creative coding is the use of shaders. Shaders are small programs that run directly on the GPU, allowing for complex and real-time visual effects. In the context of art, shaders can be thought of as brushes and paints for the digital canvas. You can use shaders to create intricate patterns, simulate natural phenomena, or produce abstract visual effects that are impossible to achieve with traditional media.

WebGL Frameworks and Libraries

To streamline the creative coding process, several WebGL frameworks and libraries are available. These tools provide abstractions and utilities to simplify complex tasks, making it easier to focus on the artistic aspects of your projects. Some popular WebGL libraries include Three.js, Babylon.js, and p5.js. These libraries provide pre-built components, 3D math utilities, and rendering abstractions to help you bring your creative visions to life.

Examples of Creative WebGL Projects

To inspire your creative endeavors, here are some examples of WebGL projects that showcase the fusion of code and art:

1. **Generative Art:** Artists use algorithms to create unique, generative artworks that evolve over time or in response to user input.
2. **Interactive Visualizations:** Data visualizations become engaging and interactive experiences when combined with WebGL. Users can explore data in 3D space, gaining new insights.
3. **Audio-Visual Experiences:** WebGL can be synchronized with audio, allowing for immersive audio-visual

performances and installations.

4. **Digital Sculptures:** Artists sculpt intricate 3D models and then manipulate them in real-time, blurring the line between physical and digital art.
5. **Abstract Visuals:** Complex shaders can produce mesmerizing abstract visuals that react to user interactions, creating a hypnotic experience.

In the following sections, we will dive deeper into the tools, techniques, and examples of creative coding and art using WebGL. Whether you're a seasoned artist or a curious developer, the world of expressive graphics with WebGL offers endless possibilities for creative exploration.

12.2. Generative Art Techniques

Generative art is a fascinating field within creative coding that involves using algorithms and code to create art that evolves, self-generates, or responds to external input. With WebGL, you can harness the power of the GPU to render complex and visually stunning generative artworks. In this section, we'll explore various techniques and concepts behind generative art using WebGL.

The Essence of Generative Art

At the core of generative art is the idea of using code to define the rules and behaviors of an artwork rather than creating it manually. This approach allows for the creation of art that can be infinitely unique, ever-evolving, and often unpredictable. Generative art blurs the line between the artist and the artwork, as the code becomes the creator, and the artist becomes a curator of the generated results.

Algorithmic Art

Generative art relies heavily on algorithms to generate visuals or animations. Algorithms are sets of instructions that determine how elements within the artwork should behave, how they should be positioned, and how they should interact. These algorithms can be simple or highly complex, producing a wide range of artistic results.

Randomness and Chaos

Randomness is often a key component of generative art. By introducing controlled randomness into the algorithms, artists can create artworks that exhibit unpredictable and organic qualities. Chaos theory, fractals, and Perlin noise are common tools used to introduce controlled chaos into generative art pieces.

Parametric Art

Parametric art involves defining parameters and variables that control various aspects of the artwork. Artists can create interactive generative art by allowing users to manipulate these parameters in real-time, altering the appearance or behavior of the artwork. WebGL's real-time rendering capabilities make it an excellent choice for creating parametric generative art that responds to user input.

Creative Coding Frameworks

To get started with generative art in WebGL, you can leverage creative coding frameworks like p5.js, Three.js, or Babylon.js. These frameworks provide a foundation for creating generative art by handling WebGL rendering, user interaction, and other essential tasks. They also offer tools for easily integrating generative algorithms into your projects.

Examples of Generative Art

Generative art can take many forms, from intricate fractal landscapes to abstract, dynamic animations. Here are a few examples of generative art concepts that you can explore:

1. **Fractal Art:** Utilizing recursive algorithms to create mesmerizing fractal patterns that exhibit self-similarity at different scales.
2. **Particle Systems:** Simulating particles with rules for movement and behavior, resulting in dynamic and evolving visual effects.
3. **L-systems:** Defining complex shapes and structures using formal grammars, which can produce intricate and branching patterns.
4. **Reaction-Diffusion:** Modeling the diffusion of substances to generate abstract and organic patterns reminiscent of natural phenomena.
5. **Cellular Automata:** Creating art through the evolution of simple cellular automata rules, often resulting in patterns reminiscent of biological growth.
6. **Procedural Generative Art:** Using procedural algorithms to generate art with parameters that can be tweaked to explore a wide range of visual possibilities.

In the subsequent sections, we will delve deeper into specific generative art techniques, explore code examples, and provide guidance on how to start creating your own generative artworks using WebGL. Generative art is a realm where experimentation and creativity thrive, offering endless opportunities to push the boundaries of digital artistic expression.

12.3. Interactive Audio-Visual Experiences

In the world of creative coding and WebGL, the integration of audio and visuals opens up exciting possibilities for interactive experiences. Combining the power of WebGL with audio processing allows developers and artists to create immersive and dynamic audio-visual artworks that respond to user input or real-time audio signals. In this section, we'll explore the concepts and techniques behind interactive audio-visual experiences.

The Symbiotic Relationship

Audio and visuals have a symbiotic relationship in interactive art. When synchronized effectively, they can enhance each other, creating a more immersive and engaging experience. The harmony between audio and visuals can convey emotions, tell stories, or provide a unique form of user interaction.

WebGL and Audio APIs

To create interactive audio-visual experiences in WebGL, you can use the Web Audio API in combination with the WebGL rendering capabilities. The Web Audio API provides tools for audio synthesis, effects processing, and real-time audio analysis. By synchronizing audio playback with WebGL rendering, you can create tightly integrated interactive experiences.

Audio Visualization

Audio visualization involves translating audio data into visual elements. You can use audio analysis techniques to extract features like amplitude, frequency, and beat information from audio signals. These features can then drive visual elements in your WebGL scene.

For example, you can make objects pulse with the beat of the music or change colors based on the audio's frequency spectrum.

Reactive Visuals

Interactive audio-visual experiences often respond to user input or real-time audio data. You can create interactive elements in your WebGL scene that users can control, such as audio filters, visual effects, or animations triggered by gestures or mouse movements. This interactivity can make the artwork more engaging and encourage user exploration.

Synchronized Storytelling

Audio and visuals can work together to tell a story or convey a message. By synchronizing audio narration with visual scenes, you can create immersive storytelling experiences. WebGL's real-time rendering capabilities enable the creation of interactive narratives where users can explore different aspects of the story at their own pace.

Code Examples

Here's a simple example of how you can integrate audio and visuals in a WebGL scene using JavaScript:

```
// Initialize the Web Audio API

const audioContext = new AudioContext();

// Load and play an audio file

const audioElement = new Audio('my_audio.mp3');

const audioSource = audioContext.createMediaElementSource(audioElement);
```

```
audioSource.connect(audioContext.destination);

audioElement.play();

// Create a WebGL scene

const canvas = document.getElementById('myCanvas');

const gl = canvas.getContext('webgl');

// Set up shaders, buffers, and rendering here

// Create a function to update visuals based on audio data

function updateVisuals() {

// Analyze audio data here and update visuals accordingly

requestAnimationFrame(updateVisuals);

}

// Start the update loop

updateVisuals();
```

This code sets up a basic integration of audio playback and WebGL rendering. You can expand on this foundation to create more complex interactive audio-visual experiences.

In the following sections, we will explore advanced techniques and examples of interactive audio-visual artworks created with WebGL, showcasing the diverse creative possibilities in this field.

12.4. The Intersection of Art and Coding

The realm of creative coding using WebGL represents the harmonious intersection of art and coding. In this section, we'll delve into the exciting fusion of artistic creativity and technical expertise, where artists and developers leverage WebGL to create visually stunning and interactive works of art.

Artistic Expression through Code

Creative coding with WebGL empowers artists to express themselves in unique and dynamic ways. Instead of traditional media, artists use code as their canvas, manipulating graphics and animations with precision. The ability to create art that responds to user interactions or external data sources adds an interactive dimension to their work.

Generative Art

Generative art is a prominent genre within creative coding. It involves writing algorithms that generate artwork procedurally. Artists can define rules and parameters, allowing the code to produce endless variations of a piece. WebGL's real-time rendering capabilities are particularly well-suited for generative art, enabling artists to create dynamic and evolving visual experiences.

Interactive Installations

WebGL has found its way into interactive art installations, blurring the boundaries between traditional art spaces and technology-driven experiences. Artists can use WebGL to create immersive and interactive installations that respond to visitors' movements, gestures, or touch. These installations often rely on sensors, cameras, and other hardware to capture user input and adapt the visual display accordingly.

Collaborative Projects

The collaborative nature of WebGL development fosters partnerships between artists and programmers. Artists can focus on the visual and conceptual aspects of a project, while developers implement the technical components. This synergy results in the creation of interactive artworks that push the boundaries of what is possible.

Accessibility and Inclusivity

Creative coding with WebGL has the potential to make art more accessible and inclusive. Interactive art installations can be designed to accommodate individuals with disabilities, providing sensory-rich experiences through alternative input methods, such as voice commands or haptic feedback.

Code as an Artistic Medium

Some artists view code as a medium in itself. The lines of code become part of the artwork, blurring the distinction between the technical and artistic aspects. In this context, the code's aesthetic and readability become crucial, as they contribute to the overall artistic expression.

Code Examples

While not providing specific code examples, it's important to emphasize that creative coding projects often involve a combination of programming languages and libraries. WebGL, JavaScript, and associated frameworks like Three.js are commonly used tools. Artists and developers work closely together to translate artistic concepts into functional code.

In the following sections, we will explore more examples of creative coding and generative art, showcasing the diverse range of artistic possibilities enabled by WebGL and coding.

The fusion of art and code in creative coding using WebGL is a testament to the boundless potential of technology in the world of artistic expression. It invites artists and developers to collaborate, innovate, and explore new frontiers in the realm of digital art.

12.5. Showcasing Creative Projects

In this section, we'll focus on the importance of showcasing creative projects created with WebGL and creative coding. Showcasing your work effectively can open up opportunities for collaboration, recognition, and even career advancement. Here, we'll explore various strategies and platforms for presenting your creative coding projects to a wider audience.

The Significance of Presentation

While the process of creating a creative coding project is immensely rewarding, sharing your work with others is equally vital. Effective presentation can transform your project from a personal endeavor into a source of inspiration for others. It can also lead to valuable feedback, collaboration opportunities, or even job offers in the creative and tech industries.

Building an Online Portfolio

One of the most common and impactful ways to showcase your creative coding projects is by creating an online portfolio. An online portfolio is a dedicated website or web page where you can display your work, describe your creative process, and provide context for each project. It serves as a digital gallery that potential collaborators, employers, or enthusiasts can explore.

Choosing the Right Platform

When building your online portfolio, you have several platform options to consider. These include personal websites, website builders, content management systems (CMS), and dedicated portfolio platforms. Each has its own advantages and level of customization. The choice largely depends on your technical skills, budget, and desired level of control.

Portfolio Content

The content of your portfolio should be carefully curated to highlight your best work. Consider including the following elements:

1. **Project Descriptions**: Provide detailed descriptions of your projects, explaining the concepts, technologies used, and the creative process behind them.
2. **Visuals**: High-quality images, screenshots, or videos that showcase your projects in action. Make sure to capture the essence of each project visually.
3. **Code Samples**: If you're comfortable sharing your code, include snippets or links to the repositories where your code is hosted. This can be especially appealing to potential collaborators or employers.
4. **Interactive Demos**: Whenever possible, offer interactive demos of your projects directly on your portfolio. This allows visitors to engage with your work firsthand.
5. **Process and Documentation**: Share insights into your creative process, challenges you've overcome, and any

documentation or research related to your projects.

Storytelling

Effective storytelling can greatly enhance the impact of your portfolio. Instead of merely listing your projects, tell a compelling narrative about your creative journey. Explain the motivation behind your work, the problems you aimed to solve, and the unique solutions you've devised. Personal anecdotes and behind-the-scenes stories can captivate your audience.

Networking and Community Engagement

Building a presence in the creative coding community can help you gain exposure and connect with like-minded individuals. Consider joining online forums, social media groups, or attending conferences and meetups related to creative coding and WebGL. Engaging with others can lead to collaborations, feedback, and opportunities you might not have encountered otherwise.

Keeping Your Portfolio Updated

Lastly, remember that your online portfolio is a dynamic entity. As you continue to create new projects and refine your skills, update your portfolio regularly to reflect your latest work. An up-to-date portfolio shows that you're actively engaged in the field and committed to growth.

By showcasing your creative coding projects effectively, you can inspire others, connect with potential collaborators, and establish yourself as a prominent figure in the intersection of art and technology. Your portfolio becomes a testament to your creativity, skill, and passion for the world of creative coding with WebGL.

Chapter 13: WebGL in Gaming

13.1. Building a Basic Game Engine

In this section, we'll dive into the exciting world of using WebGL for game development. Building a basic game engine from scratch will give you a solid foundation to create interactive and immersive 3D games. While we won't be creating a full-fledged game engine, we'll cover the essential components and concepts needed to get you started.

The Role of a Game Engine

A game engine is a software framework that simplifies and streamlines the process of creating games. It provides essential tools, libraries, and functionalities, such as rendering graphics, managing game assets, handling physics, and controlling game logic. By developing a basic game engine, you'll gain insights into how these components work together.

Setting Up Your Game Environment

Before we start building our game engine, ensure that you have a development environment with WebGL support. Most modern web browsers support WebGL, so you can use a simple HTML file to create your game. You'll also need a text editor or integrated development environment (IDE) for writing code.

Creating a Canvas

In a web-based game, the primary area for rendering graphics is an HTML5 canvas element. You can create a canvas by adding the following code to your HTML file:

```
<!DOCTYPE html>

<html>

<head>

<title>My WebGL Game</title>

</head>

<body>

<canvas id="gameCanvas" width="800" height="600"></canvas>

</body>

</html>
```

Here, we've defined a canvas element with the id "gameCanvas" and set its width and height attributes. This canvas will serve as the viewport for our game.

Initializing WebGL

To work with WebGL, you'll need to write JavaScript code. First, you'll want to get a reference to the canvas element in your JavaScript code:

```
const canvas = document.getElementById("gameCanvas");
```

Next, you'll initialize WebGL:

```
const gl = canvas.getContext("webgl");

if (!gl) {

console.error("WebGL is not supported in your browser.");

}
```

This code retrieves the WebGL rendering context and checks if it's available. If WebGL is not supported, an error message is displayed in the console.

Rendering a Basic Scene

Now that you have WebGL set up, let's render a basic scene to ensure everything is working correctly. We'll render a colored triangle on the canvas.

```
// Define the vertices of the triangle

const vertices = new Float32Array([

0.0, 1.0, 0.0,

-1.0, -1.0, 0.0,

1.0, -1.0, 0.0

]);

// Create a buffer to store the vertices

const vertexBuffer = gl.createBuffer();

gl.bindBuffer(gl.ARRAY_BUFFER, vertexBuffer);

gl.bufferData(gl.ARRAY_BUFFER, vertices,
gl.STATIC_DRAW);

// Create a vertex shader

const vertexShaderSource = `

attribute vec4 coordinates;

void main(void) {
```

```
gl_Position = coordinates;
}
`;
const vertexShader = gl.createShader(gl.VERTEX_SHADER);
gl.shaderSource(vertexShader, vertexShaderSource);
gl.compileShader(vertexShader);
// Create a fragment shader
const fragmentShaderSource = `
void main(void) {
gl_FragColor = vec4(0.0, 1.0, 0.0, 1.0);
}
`;
const fragmentShader = gl.createShader(gl.FRAGMENT_SHADER);
gl.shaderSource(fragmentShader, fragmentShaderSource);
gl.compileShader(fragmentShader);
// Create and link a shader program
const shaderProgram = gl.createProgram();
gl.attachShader(shaderProgram, vertexShader);
gl.attachShader(shaderProgram, fragmentShader);
gl.linkProgram(shaderProgram);
```

```
gl.useProgram(shaderProgram);

// Get the attribute location and enable it

const coord = gl.getAttribLocation(shaderProgram, "coordinates");

gl.enableVertexAttribArray(coord);

// Point an attribute to the currently bound VBO

gl.bindBuffer(gl.ARRAY_BUFFER, vertexBuffer);

gl.vertexAttribPointer(coord, 3, gl.FLOAT, false, 0, 0);

// Draw the triangle

gl.drawArrays(gl.TRIANGLES, 0, 3);
```

This code defines the vertices of a triangle, creates shaders for vertex and fragment processing, and renders the triangle with a green color. If everything is set up correctly, you should see a green triangle on your canvas.

Conclusion

In this section, we've started building a basic game engine using WebGL. We've set up a canvas, initialized WebGL, and rendered a simple scene. This is just the beginning; in the following sections, we'll explore more advanced game development concepts and features to create engaging 3D games.

13.2. Physics and Collision in Games

In this section, we will delve into the critical aspects of physics and collision detection in game development using WebGL. Physics simulation is a fundamental component of many games, as it enables realistic movements, interactions, and responses within the game world. Implementing physics and collision detection allows objects to interact with each other, the environment, and the player, providing a more immersive gaming experience.

The Role of Physics

Physics in games is responsible for simulating the behavior of objects within the virtual world. It encompasses various aspects such as gravity, forces, motion, collisions, and more. Implementing physics enables objects to move realistically, respond to external forces, and interact with each other.

Integrating a Physics Engine

While you can implement physics from scratch, many game developers prefer using dedicated physics engines like Cannon.js, Ammo.js, or others. These engines provide a robust framework for handling physics interactions, making it easier to create realistic movements and collisions in your game.

To use a physics engine, you typically need to include its library in your project and initialize it. Here's a simplified example of how to integrate Cannon.js, a popular JavaScript physics engine, into your WebGL game:

```
// Include Cannon.js library

<script src="cannon.js"></script>

// Initialize the physics world

const world = new CANNON.World();

world.gravity.set(0, -9.82, 0); // Set gravity (e.g., Earth's gravity)
```

```
// Create and add objects to the physics world

const sphereShape = new CANNON.Sphere(1); // Create a sphere with radius 1

const sphereBody = new CANNON.Body({ mass: 5, shape: sphereShape });

sphereBody.position.set(0, 10, 0); // Set initial position

world.addBody(sphereBody);

// Create a ground plane

const groundShape = new CANNON.Plane();

const groundBody = new CANNON.Body({ mass: 0, shape: groundShape });

world.addBody(groundBody);
```

In this example, we include Cannon.js, initialize a physics world with gravity, and create objects with shapes and properties. You can then update the physics simulation in your game loop to handle movements and collisions.

Collision Detection

Collision detection is a critical part of physics in games. It involves checking if objects are intersecting or colliding with each other. When a collision occurs, you can apply appropriate reactions, such as bouncing, damage, or triggering events.

Here's a simplified example of how to detect collisions between two objects using Cannon.js:

```
// Detect collisions between objects
```

```
const contactNormal = new CANNON.Vec3(); // Store collision normal

const distance = 1; // Define a collision distance threshold

world.addEventListener('postStep', () => {

// Check collisions

world.contacts.forEach((contact) => {

const { bi, bj } = contact;

const shapeA = bi.shape;

const shapeB = bj.shape;

if (shapeA && shapeB) {

if (shapeA.collisionResponse && shapeB.collisionResponse) {

const collided = contact.getInternalValue();

if (collided <= distance) {

// Handle collision between shapeA and shapeB

// Apply appropriate reactions here

}

}

}

});

});
```

In this code, we listen for the 'postStep' event in the physics world to check for collisions between objects. When a collision occurs, you can access the colliding shapes and apply the desired reactions.

Conclusion

Physics and collision detection are crucial aspects of game development in WebGL. By integrating a physics engine and implementing collision detection, you can create games with realistic movements and interactions. This section has provided an overview of the role of physics, integrating a physics engine, and detecting collisions, laying the foundation for more advanced game development in WebGL.

13.3. Dynamic Lighting and Effects

Dynamic lighting and effects play a significant role in enhancing the visual appeal and immersion of WebGL games. In this section, we will explore various techniques and approaches to implementing dynamic lighting and effects in your WebGL projects.

Importance of Dynamic Lighting

Dynamic lighting allows you to create realistic and engaging scenes by simulating how light interacts with objects in real-time. It adds depth, shadows, and highlights, making the game world feel more vibrant and interactive. Dynamic lighting can also be used to convey emotions, time of day, and environmental changes.

Lighting Models

To achieve dynamic lighting, WebGL developers often use lighting models that simulate how light interacts with surfaces. Common lighting models include:

• **Phong Lighting Model:** The Phong model is a popular choice for simulating diffuse, specular, and ambient lighting. It calculates the reflection of light on surfaces, resulting in highlights and shadows.

• **Blinn-Phong Lighting Model:** Similar to the Phong model, the Blinn-Phong model offers a compromise between realism and performance. It calculates lighting by considering the viewer's position.

• **Physically-Based Rendering (PBR):** PBR is a more advanced approach that takes into account the physical properties of materials, such as roughness and metallicness. It aims to achieve highly realistic lighting effects.

Implementing Dynamic Lighting

To implement dynamic lighting in WebGL, you need to consider the following aspects:

1. **Light Sources:** You must define light sources in your scene, such as directional lights, point lights, or spotlights. Each light source has specific properties like color, intensity, and position.
2. **Materials:** Assign appropriate materials to objects in your scene. Materials define how surfaces respond to light, including properties like diffuse reflection, specular reflection, and shininess.
3. **Shaders:** Create custom shaders or modify existing ones to calculate lighting effects. Shaders are responsible for determining how light interacts with objects based on their materials.

4. **Rendering Passes:** Implement multiple rendering passes, such as a depth pass and a lighting pass. A depth pass is used to determine which objects are visible, while a lighting pass calculates the illumination of each visible pixel.
5. **Shadow Mapping:** To achieve realistic shadows, consider implementing shadow mapping techniques like shadow maps or shadow volumes. These methods simulate how objects cast shadows on each other.

WebGL Libraries and Frameworks

Several WebGL libraries and frameworks can simplify the implementation of dynamic lighting and effects. Some popular options include:

- **Three.js:** Three.js is a versatile 3D graphics library that provides built-in support for dynamic lighting and materials. It offers an easy-to-use API for creating interactive 3D scenes.

- **Babylon.js:** Babylon.js is another powerful 3D engine that supports dynamic lighting and PBR materials. It offers a wide range of features for game development and simulations.

- **PlayCanvas:** PlayCanvas is a WebGL-based game engine designed for creating immersive 3D experiences. It includes a visual editor for designing scenes with dynamic lighting.

Shader Examples

Here's a simplified example of a fragment shader that implements basic Phong shading for dynamic lighting:

```
// Vertex Shader

// ...

// Fragment Shader

precision mediump float;

varying vec3 vNormal;

varying vec3 vViewDir;

uniform vec3 lightPosition;

uniform vec3 lightColor;

uniform vec3 ambientLight;

void main() {

vec3 normal = normalize(vNormal);

vec3 lightDir = normalize(lightPosition - gl_FragCoord.xyz);

vec3 viewDir = normalize(vViewDir);

// Calculate diffuse and specular components

float diffuse = max(dot(normal, lightDir), 0.0);

vec3 reflectDir = reflect(-lightDir, normal);

float specular = pow(max(dot(reflectDir, viewDir), 0.0), 32.0);

// Combine ambient, diffuse, and specular lighting
```

```
vec3 result = (ambientLight + diffuse) * lightColor + specular;

gl_FragColor = vec4(result, 1.0);

}
```

This shader calculates the lighting components for each fragment, including ambient, diffuse, and specular lighting. You can customize it further to achieve various dynamic lighting effects.

Conclusion

Dynamic lighting and effects are essential for creating visually stunning and immersive WebGL games. By understanding lighting models, implementing custom shaders, and utilizing WebGL libraries, you can take your game development to the next level. Experiment with different lighting techniques to achieve the desired mood and atmosphere in your WebGL projects.

13.4. Game AI Basics for WebGL

Game Artificial Intelligence (AI) is a crucial element in creating engaging and challenging gameplay experiences in WebGL-based games. In this section, we'll explore the fundamentals of game AI and how to implement it in your WebGL projects.

The Role of Game AI

Game AI is responsible for controlling non-player characters (NPCs) and making them behave intelligently within the game world. It adds a layer of unpredictability and challenge to the gameplay, making it more enjoyable for players. Game AI can be used for a variety of purposes, including enemy behavior, pathfinding, decision-making, and more.

Types of Game AI

There are different types of game AI, each serving a specific purpose:

1. **Finite State Machines (FSM):** FSMs are used to model NPC behavior by defining a finite number of states and transitions between them. For example, an enemy NPC might have states like "patrol," "chase," and "attack."
2. **Behavior Trees:** Behavior trees provide a more flexible way to design complex NPC behavior. They consist of nodes that represent actions or decisions and are connected in a hierarchical structure.
3. **Pathfinding Algorithms:** Pathfinding algorithms like A* are essential for NPCs to navigate the game world. They find the shortest path from one point to another while avoiding obstacles.
4. **Decision-Making Algorithms:** NPCs often need to make decisions based on their goals and the current game state. Decision-making algorithms like utility theory or rule-based systems can be employed for this purpose.

Implementing Game AI in WebGL

To implement game AI in WebGL, you'll need to consider the following steps:

1. **Define NPC Behavior:** Determine the behaviors you want your NPCs to exhibit. Create states or behaviors that cover actions like patrolling, chasing, attacking, and retreating.
2. **Create AI Logic:** Write the logic for each NPC's behavior using the chosen AI techniques. For FSMs, define states and transitions. For behavior trees, create the tree structure. For pathfinding, implement algorithms to find

paths.

3. **Integrate with Game Logic:** Integrate the AI logic with your game's overall logic. NPCs should respond to events in the game, such as player actions or changes in the environment.
4. **Testing and Tweaking:** Test your game AI extensively to ensure that NPCs behave as expected. Adjust parameters and behaviors as needed to achieve the desired level of challenge and fun.

WebGL AI Libraries

Several JavaScript libraries can help you implement game AI in WebGL-based games. Some popular options include:

- **A-Frame:** A-Frame is a web framework for building virtual reality experiences. It includes components for creating interactive and AI-controlled entities in VR environments.

- **Babylon.js:** Babylon.js provides support for AI features like pathfinding and behavior trees. It's suitable for creating complex AI-driven NPCs in WebGL games.

- **Three.js:** Three.js, while primarily a 3D graphics library, can be combined with other JavaScript AI libraries to implement AI in WebGL projects.

AI Examples

Here's a simplified example of an FSM-based AI for an enemy NPC in WebGL:

```
class EnemyAI {
```

```
constructor() {
this.state = "patrol";
}
update() {
switch (this.state) {
case "patrol":
// Implement patrol behavior
break;
case "chase":
// Implement chase behavior
break;
case "attack":
// Implement attack behavior
break;
}
}
setState(newState) {
this.state = newState;
}
}
```

This AI class defines different states for the enemy NPC and updates its behavior based on the current state.

Conclusion

Game AI is a vital component of WebGL-based games, enhancing gameplay by providing intelligent NPC behavior. Understanding the types of AI and how to implement them, along with using suitable libraries, will help you create immersive and challenging gaming experiences for your players. Experiment with different AI techniques to make your WebGL games stand out.

13.5. Crafting Immersive Game Environments

Creating immersive game environments is a key aspect of game development in WebGL. In this section, we'll delve into various techniques and considerations for crafting immersive worlds that captivate players and enhance their gaming experience.

Visual Realism

One of the primary goals in building immersive game environments is achieving visual realism. Realistic graphics and detailed textures can transport players into a game world. Here are some techniques to consider:

- **High-Quality Textures:** Use high-resolution textures to add fine details to objects and surfaces in your game world. These textures can be created using tools like Substance Painter or by capturing real-world textures.

- **Advanced Lighting:** Implement advanced lighting techniques such as physically based rendering (PBR), global illumination, and high-dynamic-range (HDR) lighting. These techniques simulate real-world lighting conditions and create more convincing environments.

- **Environmental Effects:** Add environmental effects like weather, time of day, and dynamic lighting changes to make your game world feel dynamic and alive. Weather effects like rain, fog, and snow can significantly enhance immersion.

Interactive Elements

Interactivity is another crucial element in crafting immersive game environments. Players should feel like they can interact with the world around them. Here are some considerations:

- **Physics Simulation:** Implement physics engines to create realistic object interactions. This allows objects to respond to gravity, collisions, and player actions.

- **Environmental Interactions:** Design environments that respond to player actions. For example, players should be able to open doors, push objects, or break barriers.

- **NPC Behavior:** Ensure that non-player characters (NPCs) in the game world behave realistically and respond to the player's presence and actions.

Sound and Music

Sound design plays a significant role in immersion. High-quality sound effects and music can evoke emotions and enhance the atmosphere of your game. Consider the following:

- **Ambient Sound:** Include ambient sounds that match the environment. For instance, a forest should have chirping birds and rustling leaves, while a bustling city should have traffic and chatter.

- **Dynamic Music:** Implement dynamic music systems that change based on the player's actions or the mood of the game. This creates a more responsive and immersive soundtrack.

Storytelling and Narrative

An engaging storyline and well-developed characters can draw players into the game world. Consider these storytelling techniques:

- **Character Development:** Create compelling characters with backstories, motivations, and personalities. Players should care about these characters and their fates.

- **World Building:** Develop a rich lore and history for your game world. This adds depth and believability to the environment.

- **Player Agency:** Allow players to make meaningful choices that impact the story and world. This makes players feel like they have a stake in the game's outcome.

Performance Optimization

While striving for visual realism and interactivity, it's essential to maintain good performance. Immersive environments should run smoothly on various devices. Consider these optimization techniques:

- **Level of Detail (LOD):** Implement LOD systems to reduce the level of detail for distant objects, improving performance without sacrificing visual quality.

- **Culling:** Use occlusion culling and frustum culling to avoid rendering objects that are not visible to the player.

- **Asset Streaming:** Implement asset streaming to load assets dynamically as needed, reducing initial loading times.

Conclusion

Crafting immersive game environments in WebGL requires a combination of artistic creativity, technical expertise, and attention to detail. By focusing on visual realism, interactivity, sound design, storytelling, and performance optimization, you can create game worlds that transport players to new and exciting adventures, enhancing their overall gaming experience. Experimentation and iteration are key to achieving the perfect balance between immersion and performance in your WebGL games.

14. Data Visualization with WebGL

Data visualization is a powerful tool for understanding complex information, and WebGL can be leveraged to create interactive 3D data visualizations that engage and inform users. In this chapter, we'll explore the principles and techniques of 3D data visualization using WebGL.

14.1. Principles of 3D Data Visualization

Effective data visualization goes beyond simply displaying data; it aims to convey insights, patterns, and trends in a visually intuitive manner. When working with 3D data visualization, several principles should guide your approach:

1. Understand Your Data

Before diving into visualization, it's essential to have a deep understanding of the data you're working with. This includes knowing the data's structure, variables,, and any relevant domain knowledge. Understanding the data's context will help you make informed decisions during the visualization process.

2. Choose the Right Representation

Selecting the appropriate visualization method is crucial. In 3D data visualization, this involves deciding how to represent data points and relationships in a 3D space. Common representations include scatter plots, surface plots, and volumetric rendering, among others. The choice should align with the data's characteristics and the insights you want to convey.

3. Effective Use of Color

Color is a powerful tool for encoding information in visualizations. However, it should be used judiciously. Ensure that color choices are meaningful and avoid using excessive colors, which can lead to confusion. Consider colorblind accessibility when designing visualizations.

4. Interaction and Exploration

Interactivity is a key feature of 3D data visualization. Users should be able to interact with the visualization to explore the data further. Implement controls for panning, zooming, rotating, and filtering data points. Tooltips and hover effects can provide additional context.

5. Maintain Clarity

While 3D visualizations offer depth and complexity, it's important to strike a balance between depth and clarity. Overly complex visualizations can overwhelm users and obscure insights. Aim for a balance that conveys information effectively without unnecessary complexity.

6. Performance Optimization

3D data visualizations can be computationally intensive, especially with large datasets. Optimize rendering performance by using techniques like level of detail (LOD), occlusion culling, and data streaming. Ensure that the visualization remains responsive even with extensive data.

Example: Scatter Plot in WebGL

To illustrate these principles, let's consider a simple example: creating a 3D scatter plot in WebGL. We'll use WebGL's capabilities to represent data points in 3D space, allowing users to explore the data interactively.

```
// WebGL code for a 3D scatter plot

// Initialize WebGL context and shaders

const canvas = document.getElementById("scatter-plot-canvas");

const gl = canvas.getContext("webgl");

// Load and preprocess data

const data = preprocessData(rawData);

// Create vertex and fragment shaders

const vertexShaderSource = `

// Vertex shader code

attribute vec3 position;

void main(void) {

gl_Position = vec4(position, 1.0);

}

`;

const fragmentShaderSource = `

// Fragment shader code
```

```
void main(void) {

gl_FragColor = vec4(0.0, 0.0, 1.0, 1.0); // Blue color

}

`;

// Compile and link shaders, create buffers, and render

// (Code for shader compilation, buffer creation, and rendering goes here)
```

In this example, we initialize WebGL, preprocess the data, create vertex and fragment shaders, and set up the rendering process. This is just a simplified outline, and creating a fully interactive scatter plot would involve more code and additional WebGL features.

In summary, 3D data visualization with WebGL combines data analysis, artistic design, and technical implementation. By following the principles outlined above and leveraging WebGL's capabilities, you can create informative and engaging visualizations that unlock insights from complex datasets.

14.2. Interactive Graphs and Charts

In the realm of 3D data visualization with WebGL, interactive graphs and charts play a pivotal role in conveying complex data in an understandable manner. They allow users to explore datasets, identify trends, and gain insights. This section delves into creating interactive graphs and charts using WebGL.

Understanding Interactive Graphs

Interactive graphs and charts are dynamic representations of data that enable users to interact with the visualized information. These visualizations can be customized and manipulated by users to focus on specific data points or timeframes. Common examples of interactive graphs include line charts, bar graphs, and pie charts.

WebGL for Interactive Graphs

WebGL provides a powerful platform for creating interactive 3D graphs and charts. It leverages hardware acceleration to render complex visualizations smoothly. When creating interactive graphs in WebGL, consider the following aspects:

1. **Data Binding**: WebGL graphs and charts require data binding, where data points are linked to graphical elements. The data should update the visualization in real-time, allowing for dynamic changes.
2. **User Interaction**: Implement user interaction features such as zooming, panning, and tooltip display. These interactions enhance the user's ability to explore the data and extract meaningful insights.
3. **Transitions**: Smooth transitions between data states can improve the user experience. For example, when switching between different datasets or time periods, gradual transitions can make changes less abrupt.

Example: Interactive Line Chart

Let's explore a simplified example of creating an interactive line chart in WebGL. We'll use WebGL to draw a line chart and provide user interaction for zooming and panning.

// WebGL code for an interactive line chart

// (Initialization and shader setup code)

// Load and preprocess data

```
const data = preprocessData(rawData);

// Define data-to-screen coordinate mapping functions

function mapX(dataX) {

// Map dataX to screenX

// (Implement the mapping function here)

}

function mapY(dataY) {

// Map dataY to screenY

// (Implement the mapping function here)

}

// Implement zoom and pan interactions

// (Code for zooming and panning interactions goes here)

// Render the line chart based on the data

// (Code for rendering the line chart goes here)
```

In this example, we initialize WebGL, preprocess the data, set up data-to-screen coordinate mapping functions, and implement zooming and panning interactions. The actual code for rendering the line chart would involve creating vertices and rendering primitives.

Interactive graphs and charts in WebGL provide a powerful means to convey complex data and allow users to explore it interactively. By incorporating user-friendly interactions and responsive transitions, you can create compelling data visualizations that facilitate data analysis and decision-making.

14.3. Visualizing Large Data Sets

Visualizing large data sets in WebGL presents unique challenges and opportunities. Handling a substantial amount of data efficiently while maintaining smooth performance is crucial. In this section, we'll explore techniques for visualizing large data sets effectively.

Data Aggregation and Sampling

One approach to dealing with large data sets is data aggregation. Instead of displaying every data point, you can group data into meaningful clusters or categories. For example, in a geographical data visualization, you might aggregate data by regions or cities to reduce the number of data points rendered on the screen.

Sampling is another technique that involves selecting a subset of data points to represent the entire dataset. Random or stratified sampling methods can help reduce the data's complexity while preserving its statistical characteristics.

Level of Detail (LOD) Techniques

Level of Detail (LOD) techniques involve displaying different levels of detail based on the user's viewpoint. As the user zooms in or out, the visualization adapts by showing more or fewer details. LOD can significantly improve performance when dealing with large data sets.

In WebGL, LOD can be implemented by precomputing multiple versions of data representation, such as different levels of simplification for 3D models or varying resolutions for geographical data. When the user interacts with the visualization, the appropriate LOD version is selected and displayed.

Data Streaming and Progressive Loading

For extremely large data sets that cannot be loaded entirely at once, data streaming and progressive loading techniques can be employed. Data is loaded in chunks, prioritizing the most relevant portions based on the user's viewpoint. This approach ensures that the user can interact with the visualization immediately while additional data is fetched in the background.

Example: Progressive Loading of Geographic Data

Let's consider an example of progressive loading for a geographic data visualization. Suppose you are visualizing a world map with numerous data points, and loading all data at once would be impractical due to its size. You can implement progressive loading as follows:

```
// WebGL code for progressive loading of geographic data

// (Initialization and shader setup code)

// Load an initial subset of data

const initialData = loadInitialData();

// Render the initial data

// (Code for rendering initial data goes here)

// Implement progressive loading

function loadMoreData() {

// Fetch the next batch of data

const nextDataBatch = fetchNextDataBatch();
```

```
// Render the new data

// (Code for rendering new data goes here)

}

// Set up event listeners for user interaction

// (Code for handling user interactions goes here)
```

In this example, we load an initial subset of data, render it, and then implement a function to load and render additional data when the user requests it. This allows for a smooth user experience when dealing with large datasets.

Visualizing large data sets in WebGL requires careful consideration of performance optimizations, data simplification, and user interaction. By employing techniques like data aggregation, LOD, and progressive loading, you can create responsive and informative visualizations even with massive datasets.

14.4. Real-time Data Updates

Real-time data updates are essential for certain types of WebGL data visualizations, especially those that need to reflect changes as they occur. Whether you're creating a live dashboard, monitoring system, or any other application that relies on up-to-the-minute data, implementing real-time updates can greatly enhance the user experience.

WebSocket Communication

One of the most common ways to achieve real-time data updates in WebGL is through WebSocket communication. WebSockets provide a full-duplex communication channel over a single TCP connection, making them ideal for real-time applications. You can establish a WebSocket connection between the client (browser) and a server to exchange data efficiently.

Here's a simplified example of setting up a WebSocket connection in JavaScript:

```
// Establish a WebSocket connection

const socket = new WebSocket('ws://example.com');

// Define event handlers for WebSocket events

socket.addEventListener('open', (event) => {

console.log('WebSocket connection established.');

});

socket.addEventListener('message', (event) => {

const data = JSON.parse(event.data);

console.log('Received data:', data);

// Update WebGL visualization with new data

updateVisualization(data);

});

socket.addEventListener('close', (event) => {

if (event.wasClean) {

console.log('WebSocket connection closed cleanly.');

} else {
```

```
console.error('WebSocket connection abruptly closed.');
}
});
socket.addEventListener('error', (error) => {
console.error('WebSocket error:', error);
});
```

In this example, a WebSocket connection is established, and event listeners are used to handle various WebSocket events, including the reception of new data. When new data arrives, it can be used to update the WebGL visualization accordingly.

Server-Sent Events (SSE)

Another approach for real-time updates is Server-Sent Events (SSE). SSE is a unidirectional communication channel from the server to the client over a single HTTP connection. It's simpler to set up than WebSockets when you only need to send updates from the server to the client.

Here's a basic example of using SSE in JavaScript:

```
// Create an EventSource for Server-Sent Events
const eventSource = new EventSource('/events');
// Define an event handler for incoming events
eventSource.onmessage = (event) => {
const data = JSON.parse(event.data);
console.log('Received data:', data);
```

```
// Update WebGL visualization with new data
updateVisualization(data);
};
```

In this example, the client establishes an EventSource connection to a server endpoint that sends updates as Server-Sent Events. When an event is received, the provided event handler processes the data and updates the WebGL visualization.

Real-Time Data Visualization Example

Imagine you are creating a real-time weather monitoring application with a WebGL visualization of weather patterns. You can use WebSocket or SSE to receive updates from a weather data server and continuously update the WebGL representation of weather conditions.

Implementing real-time data updates in WebGL enhances the interactivity and usefulness of your applications. Whether you choose WebSockets or SSE, the ability to display live data ensures that your visualizations remain relevant and informative in dynamic environments.

14.5. Case Studies in WebGL Data Visualization

In this section, we'll explore several case studies of real-world WebGL data visualization projects. These examples showcase the versatility and power of WebGL when applied to different domains and data visualization challenges.

1. Climate Data Visualization

One common use case for WebGL data visualization is climate data analysis. Climate scientists and researchers often need to visualize vast datasets of temperature, precipitation, and other climate-related variables. WebGL's ability to render large datasets efficiently makes it a valuable tool for exploring climate patterns and trends.

In such projects, WebGL can be used to create interactive maps and visualizations that allow users to explore historical climate data, simulate future climate scenarios, and understand the impact of climate change.

2. Financial Data Visualization

Financial institutions and traders rely on real-time data visualization to make informed decisions. WebGL can be employed to create visually compelling and interactive financial dashboards that display stock prices, market trends, and portfolio performance in real time.

These applications often involve rendering candlestick charts, line graphs, and heatmaps to represent financial data. WebGL's GPU acceleration ensures smooth and responsive interactions, even when dealing with large datasets and complex charting components.

3. Medical Imaging

Medical professionals use WebGL for visualizing and analyzing medical imaging data, such as MRI and CT scans. WebGL's ability to render 3D volumes and provide interactive tools for segmentation and analysis makes it a valuable tool in the field of medical imaging.

In medical applications, WebGL enables real-time rendering of 3D reconstructions of patient anatomy, helping doctors visualize and plan surgeries, diagnose diseases, and track treatment progress.

Interactive features like slicing, zooming, and annotating enhance the usability of these applications.

4. Geospatial Data Visualization

Geospatial data visualization involves displaying geographic and spatial data. WebGL is particularly well-suited for creating interactive maps, geographical information systems (GIS), and geospatial analysis tools. These applications can range from visualizing city infrastructure to tracking the spread of diseases on a global scale.

By leveraging WebGL's capabilities, developers can create maps that provide detailed information on terrain, land use, population density, and more. Users can zoom in, pan, and interact with map layers to gain insights and make informed decisions.

5. Scientific Simulations

Scientists and researchers use WebGL to visualize the results of scientific simulations and experiments. Whether it's simulating fluid dynamics, modeling molecular structures, or exploring astrophysical phenomena, WebGL allows scientists to represent complex data in an understandable and interactive manner.

In scientific simulations, WebGL visualizations help researchers analyze and interpret their data more effectively. Interactive 3D models and simulations aid in conveying complex scientific concepts to a broader audience.

These case studies demonstrate how WebGL can be applied to diverse fields and data visualization challenges. WebGL's ability to handle large datasets, create interactive visuals, and harness the power of the GPU makes it a valuable technology for addressing complex data visualization requirements across various domains.

15.1. The Evolving Web Ecosystem

In this section, we will explore the evolving landscape of the web ecosystem and its impact on WebGL. The web has undergone significant transformations since WebGL's inception, and understanding these changes is essential for anyone working with 3D graphics on the web.

The Rise of Web Technologies

Over the years, web technologies have evolved rapidly, enabling more sophisticated and interactive web experiences. HTML5, CSS3, and JavaScript have become more powerful and capable, providing the foundation for building complex web applications. WebGL emerged as a critical component in this evolution, allowing developers to harness the GPU for high-performance 3D graphics.

Mobile-First Approach

The shift toward mobile-first web development has been one of the defining trends in recent years. As more users access the web via smartphones and tablets, websites and applications must prioritize mobile responsiveness and performance. WebGL has adapted to this trend, with optimizations for mobile devices and support for touch and gesture controls.

WebAssembly and Performance

WebAssembly (Wasm) has emerged as a game-changer for web development. It is a binary instruction format that runs at near-native speed in web browsers, enabling developers to bring high-performance applications to the web. WebGL applications can benefit from WebAssembly to further enhance rendering performance and unlock new possibilities.

Progressive Web Apps (PWAs)

Progressive Web Apps (PWAs) have gained popularity as they offer a more app-like experience on the web. PWAs are installable, responsive, and work offline, making them a compelling choice for various web applications. WebGL can be integrated into PWAs to create immersive 3D experiences that function seamlessly across devices.

WebXR and Virtual Reality

The advent of WebXR has paved the way for virtual and augmented reality experiences on the web. With WebXR, developers can create VR and AR applications that run directly in the browser, leveraging WebGL for rendering 3D content. This has opened up new possibilities for web-based virtual reality and augmented reality applications.

The Future of Web Graphics

Looking ahead, the web ecosystem is likely to continue evolving. Emerging technologies, such as WebGPU and real-time ray tracing, promise even more advanced graphics capabilities on the web. Developers working with WebGL should stay updated with these developments to leverage the latest tools and techniques.

Conclusion

As the web ecosystem evolves, WebGL remains a crucial technology for delivering immersive 3D graphics and interactive experiences.

Developers should adapt to changes in web technologies, embrace mobile-first strategies, explore WebAssembly for performance improvements, consider PWAs for enhanced user experiences, and explore the potential of WebXR for virtual and augmented reality applications. By staying informed and adaptable, developers can continue to push the boundaries of what's possible with WebGL on the web.

15.2. Emerging Trends in 3D Web Graphics

In this section, we will delve into the emerging trends and developments in the field of 3D web graphics. The web continues to evolve, and staying abreast of these trends is vital for web developers and WebGL enthusiasts.

Real-time Ray Tracing

Real-time ray tracing is one of the most significant advancements in 3D graphics. Traditionally used in offline rendering, ray tracing can now be achieved in real-time, thanks to hardware acceleration and optimized algorithms. This technology enables more realistic lighting, shadows, and reflections, enhancing the visual quality of WebGL applications.

```
// Example of WebGL code using real-time ray tracing techniques

const canvas = document.getElementById('webgl-canvas');

const gl = canvas.getContext('webgl2');

// Set up ray tracing shaders and buffers

const rayTracingProgram = initRayTracingProgram(gl);

const rayTracingBuffers = initRayTracingBuffers(gl);
```

```
// Render the scene using ray tracing
function render() {
gl.useProgram(rayTracingProgram);
// Bind ray tracing buffers and textures
bindRayTracingResources(gl, rayTracingProgram, rayTracingBuffers);
// Perform ray tracing calculations
rayTraceScene(gl);
// Render the final image on the canvas
renderToCanvas(gl, rayTracingBuffers);
requestAnimationFrame(render);
}
render();
```

WebGPU Integration

WebGPU is an emerging graphics and compute API that promises to provide low-level access to GPU capabilities in web applications. It aims to be a more modern and efficient replacement for WebGL, offering better performance and flexibility. Developers should keep an eye on WebGPU as it matures and becomes more widely adopted.

```
// Example of using WebGPU in a WebGL application
const canvas = document.getElementById('webgl-canvas');
const adapter = await navigator.gpu.requestAdapter();
```

```
const device = await adapter.requestDevice();

const context = canvas.getContext('gpupresent');

// Create WebGPU resources and perform rendering

// (WebGPU code can coexist with WebGL code in the same application)
```

Web3D and the Metaverse

The concept of the metaverse, a shared virtual space where users interact with each other and digital content, has gained significant attention. Web3D technologies, including WebGL, play a crucial role in building the metaverse. Developers are exploring ways to create interconnected 3D experiences on the web, fostering social interactions and immersive environments.

Cross-Platform Compatibility

With the proliferation of devices and platforms, ensuring cross-platform compatibility is essential. WebGL applications must be accessible and functional across various browsers, operating systems, and devices. Techniques such as responsive design and progressive enhancement are crucial for delivering consistent experiences.

Art and Web-Integrated Experiences

WebGL has also found its place in the world of art and creative coding. Artists and designers are increasingly using WebGL to create interactive and visually stunning web experiences. These projects often blur the lines between art and technology, resulting in captivating digital artworks.

```
// Example of a creative WebGL project

const canvas = document.getElementById('webgl-canvas');

const gl = canvas.getContext('webgl2');

// Create custom shaders and textures

const vertexShaderSource = `

// Vertex shader code

`;

const fragmentShaderSource = `

// Fragment shader code

`;

const shaderProgram = createShaderProgram(gl,
vertexShaderSource, fragmentShaderSource);

// Define and render unique 3D scenes

const scene = createCustomWebGLScene(gl);

// Implement interactivity and user engagement

setupInteractiveFeatures(canvas, scene);

// Render the scene

scene.render();
```

Accessibility and Inclusivity

As WebGL content becomes more prevalent, ensuring accessibility for all users is crucial. Developers should follow accessibility best practices, including providing alternative content for non-visual users and making interactive 3D elements navigable via keyboard and screen readers.

In conclusion, the world of 3D web graphics is continually evolving, and developers should remain adaptable to embrace these emerging trends. Whether it's harnessing real-time ray tracing, exploring WebGPU, contributing to the metaverse, ensuring cross-platform compatibility, creating artful experiences, or prioritizing accessibility, WebGL enthusiasts have an exciting future ahead. By staying informed and experimenting with these trends, developers can contribute to the growth and innovation of 3D web graphics.

15.3. WebGL and WebAssembly

In this section, we will explore the integration of WebGL with WebAssembly, a powerful technology that allows developers to run high-performance, low-level code directly in web browsers. The combination of WebGL and WebAssembly opens up new possibilities for web-based 3D graphics and applications.

WebAssembly Overview

WebAssembly, often abbreviated as WASM, is a binary instruction format designed for safe and efficient execution on web browsers. It serves as a compilation target for high-level programming languages like C, C++, and Rust. WebAssembly code can run at near-native speed, making it suitable for computationally intensive tasks, such as 3D rendering and physics simulations.

To use WebAssembly with WebGL, developers typically compile their C/C++ or Rust code to WASM bytecode and load it alongside JavaScript. This bytecode is executed by the browser's WebAssembly virtual machine, providing a bridge between JavaScript and low-level code.

```
// Example of loading and using WebAssembly in a JavaScript file

fetch('example.wasm')

.then(response => response.arrayBuffer())

.then(bytes => WebAssembly.instantiate(bytes, {}))

.then(result => {

const exports = result.instance.exports;

// Access and call WebAssembly functions from JavaScript

const result = exports.myWebAssemblyFunction();

console.log(result);

});
```

WebGL and WebAssembly Integration

The integration of WebGL and WebAssembly can yield several benefits:

1. **Performance**: WebAssembly code can execute complex calculations significantly faster than equivalent JavaScript, making it ideal for performance-critical tasks in WebGL applications.
2. **Compatibility**: WebAssembly is designed to work seamlessly with existing web technologies, allowing WebGL and WebAssembly to coexist in the same web page.
3. **Code Reusability**: Developers can reuse existing C/C++

or Rust codebases by compiling them to WebAssembly, reducing the need to rewrite algorithms for the web.

4. **Interactivity**: WebAssembly can enable real-time physics simulations, AI algorithms, and other computationally intensive features in WebGL applications, enhancing interactivity.

```
// Example of using WebAssembly for physics simulations in a WebGL application

const canvas = document.getElementById('webgl-canvas');

const gl = canvas.getContext('webgl2');

// Load and instantiate the physics simulation WebAssembly module

fetch('physics.wasm')

.then(response => response.arrayBuffer())

.then(bytes => WebAssembly.instantiate(bytes, {}))

.then(result => {

const physicsModule = result.instance.exports;

// Initialize the physics simulation

physicsModule.initSimulation();

// Render loop

function render() {

// Update physics simulation

physicsModule.updateSimulation();
```

```
// Render the scene
renderScene(gl);
requestAnimationFrame(render);
}
render(); // Start the rendering loop
});
```

Use Cases

WebAssembly can be particularly beneficial in WebGL applications when dealing with complex simulations, procedural generation, pathfinding algorithms, and other computationally expensive tasks. It allows developers to create more sophisticated and responsive 3D experiences without sacrificing performance.

Moreover, by combining WebGL and WebAssembly, developers can leverage the full power of the GPU for rendering while using WebAssembly for non-graphical computations. This hybrid approach can lead to highly optimized and responsive web applications, especially in fields like gaming, scientific visualization, and simulations.

In summary, the integration of WebGL and WebAssembly represents a promising direction for web-based 3D graphics development. It enables developers to harness the performance benefits of WebAssembly while still utilizing the expressive capabilities of WebGL for rendering. As these technologies continue to evolve, we can expect to see more innovative and performance-driven web-based 3D applications and games.

15.4. Future Challenges and Opportunities

As we look ahead to the future of WebGL, several challenges and opportunities emerge. WebGL has come a long way since its inception, but there is still much room for growth and innovation. In this section, we'll explore some of the key areas where WebGL is likely to evolve and the opportunities it presents for developers.

1. Performance Optimization

Performance optimization will continue to be a focal point for WebGL developers. As web browsers and hardware become more capable, expectations for smooth and immersive 3D experiences will rise. Developers will need to employ advanced techniques, such as level-of-detail rendering, to balance graphical quality with performance.

2. WebGPU Integration

WebGPU is an emerging standard that aims to provide low-level, high-performance access to GPU hardware, similar to WebAssembly but tailored specifically for graphics. The integration of WebGPU with WebGL could lead to even more efficient and powerful web-based 3D graphics.

3. VR and AR Integration

The lines between virtual reality (VR) and augmented reality (AR) are blurring, and WebGL will play a significant role in both. With the growth of WebXR (Web Extended Reality) standards, developers can create immersive VR and AR experiences directly in web browsers, making it more accessible and user-friendly.

4. Web3D and Decentralized Applications (dApps)

Web3D is an exciting frontier that combines 3D graphics with blockchain technology. Decentralized applications (dApps) can benefit from WebGL by creating visually engaging user interfaces and interactive 3D elements within blockchain-powered environments.

5. WebGL in Education

WebGL has great potential in educational contexts, enabling interactive 3D simulations, scientific visualizations, and engaging learning experiences. As web-based education continues to grow, WebGL can enhance the quality of online educational content.

6. Cross-Platform Compatibility

Ensuring that WebGL applications work smoothly across different web browsers and devices remains a challenge. Developers will need to invest in testing and compatibility solutions to reach the broadest audience.

7. WebGL Community and Resources

The WebGL community is vital for knowledge sharing, collaboration, and support. As more developers join the community, resources like forums, tutorials, and open-source projects will continue to grow, providing valuable tools and insights.

8. WebGL Accessibility

Making WebGL content accessible to individuals with disabilities is an important consideration. Ensuring that 3D graphics can be navigated and understood through assistive technologies will be crucial for inclusive web experiences.

9. Environmental Impact

The environmental impact of 3D graphics, especially in web-based gaming, is a growing concern. Developers will need to explore sustainable practices and optimizations to reduce the energy consumption of WebGL applications.

10. Emerging Technologies

The rapid pace of technological innovation introduces new possibilities for WebGL. This includes advancements in real-time ray tracing, machine learning integration, and immersive haptic feedback—all of which can enhance the realism and interactivity of web-based 3D graphics.

In conclusion, WebGL has a bright future filled with exciting challenges and opportunities. As it continues to evolve alongside web technologies, hardware capabilities, and developer expertise, we can expect increasingly immersive and engaging 3D experiences on the web. Whether you're a seasoned WebGL developer or just starting, the journey ahead promises innovation, creativity, and the chance to shape the future of web-based 3D graphics.

15.5. Preparing for the Next Wave in Web Graphics

As we wrap up our exploration of WebGL and its future, it's important to reflect on the broader context of web graphics and the direction in which the web is heading. WebGL is just one piece of the puzzle in the ever-evolving landscape of web technologies. In this section, we'll discuss how WebGL fits into the larger ecosystem and how you can prepare for the next wave in web graphics.

1. WebGL and WebAssembly

WebGL and WebAssembly are two complementary technologies that can work hand-in-hand. While WebGL is focused on graphics rendering, WebAssembly allows you to run high-performance, low-level code in the browser. As these technologies continue to mature, consider leveraging their combined power for more ambitious web projects.

2. WebGL and WebXR

WebXR, or Web Extended Reality, is the future of immersive experiences on the web. It encompasses virtual reality (VR) and augmented reality (AR) and provides APIs for building immersive 3D worlds. Familiarize yourself with WebXR standards and how they integrate with WebGL to create compelling VR and AR applications.

3. 3D Web Standards

WebGL is just one part of the broader ecosystem of 3D web standards. Familiarize yourself with related standards like glTF (a file format for 3D models) and the WebXR Device API. These standards ensure interoperability and compatibility across the 3D web.

4. Progressive Web Apps (PWAs)

Progressive Web Apps are web applications that provide a native app-like experience on the web. Integrating WebGL into PWAs can lead to engaging and performant web applications. Explore the possibilities of PWAs to deliver 3D experiences to users across different devices.

5. WebGL and Mobile Devices

Mobile devices are a dominant platform for web usage. Ensure that your WebGL applications are responsive and perform well on smartphones and tablets. Mobile optimization is essential for reaching a broader audience.

6. WebGL and Web3.0

Web3.0 represents the next phase of the internet, where blockchain, decentralized applications (dApps), and digital currencies play a significant role. WebGL can be integrated into the web3.0 ecosystem by creating visually engaging and interactive dApps.

7. Continuous Learning and Experimentation

The web is a dynamic environment, and technologies evolve rapidly. To stay relevant, embrace a mindset of continuous learning and experimentation. Keep up with the latest developments in WebGL, graphics programming, and web standards.

8. Community Engagement

Engage with the WebGL and web development communities. Attend conferences, participate in forums, and collaborate on open-source projects. Networking and sharing knowledge with fellow developers can lead to new insights and opportunities.

9. Ethical and Inclusive Design

As web graphics become more immersive and interactive, consider the ethical implications of your work. Strive for inclusive design that considers accessibility, diversity, and environmental impact.

10. Exploration and Creativity

Finally, don't forget the power of creativity. WebGL offers a canvas for artistic expression and innovative storytelling. Push the boundaries of what's possible in web graphics, experiment with unconventional ideas, and create memorable user experiences.

In conclusion, WebGL is a remarkable technology that has transformed web graphics and 3D experiences. As you prepare for the next wave in web graphics, keep in mind the broader context of web technologies, emerging standards, and the evolving needs of users. By staying curious, adaptable, and engaged with the web development community, you can play an active role in shaping the future of web graphics and creating experiences that captivate and inspire.

Chapter 16: Building a WebGL Portfolio

In this chapter, we'll explore the process of building a WebGL portfolio to showcase your skills and projects. A portfolio is a crucial tool for any WebGL developer, as it not only demonstrates your expertise but also helps you stand out in the competitive world of web graphics. Whether you're a student looking to start your career or a professional aiming to attract clients and employers, creating an impressive WebGL portfolio is a valuable endeavor.

16.1. Planning Your Portfolio Projects

Before you start assembling your portfolio, it's essential to plan your projects strategically. Here are some key considerations:

Define Your Goals:

- Determine the purpose of your portfolio. Are you seeking employment, freelance opportunities, or personal branding?

Showcase a Range:

- Include a variety of projects that highlight your versatility. This could include 3D games, interactive simulations, data visualizations, or artistic experiments.

Quality Over Quantity:

- It's better to have a few polished projects than a large quantity of mediocre ones. Focus on projects that demonstrate your skills and creativity effectively.

Tell a Story:

- Craft a narrative for each project. Explain the problem or concept, your approach, and the impact or results.

Include Personal Projects:

- Personal projects can reveal your passion and initiative. They also provide opportunities to experiment and innovate.

16.2. Effective Presentation of 3D Work

Presentation is key to a successful WebGL portfolio. Here's how to make your projects shine:

High-Quality Screenshots:

- Capture high-resolution screenshots of your projects from multiple angles. These images serve as the first impression of your work.

Interactive Demos:

- Whenever possible, provide live demos of your projects. Allow visitors to interact with your 3D scenes directly in their browsers.

Videos and GIFs:

- Record short videos or create GIFs to showcase dynamic or interactive aspects of your projects. This helps convey the user experience.

Project Descriptions:

- Write detailed descriptions for each project. Explain the context, challenges, and technologies used. Use concise language and avoid jargon.

Source Code:

- If you're comfortable sharing your code, include links to your GitHub or repository. This can demonstrate your coding skills and transparency.

16.3. Building an Online Presence

A strong online presence can attract more attention to your portfolio. Consider these tips:

Portfolio Website:

- Create a dedicated website for your portfolio. It adds professionalism and gives you more control over the presentation.

Blog or Articles:

- Share your knowledge and insights by writing blog posts or articles related to WebGL or 3D graphics. This positions you as an expert in the field.

Social Media:

- Share your projects and engage with the WebGL and web development communities on platforms like Twitter, LinkedIn, and GitHub.

Online Communities:

- Participate in forums, discussion boards, and online communities related to WebGL. Offer help, share your work, and learn from others.

16.4. Networking and Community Involvement

Networking is essential for career growth. Here's how to connect with others in the industry:

Attend Conferences and Meetups:

- Attend WebGL-related conferences, meetups, and events. These gatherings offer opportunities to meet potential employers, collaborators, and mentors.

Join Online Groups:

- Become a member of WebGL-related online groups and forums. Contribute to discussions and share your knowledge.

Collaborate:

- Collaborate on open-source projects, side projects, or freelance work. Working with others can broaden your experience and network.

16.5. Finding Opportunities in WebGL Development

Once your portfolio is ready and you've established your online presence, it's time to explore career opportunities. Here are some avenues to consider:

Job Search:

- Look for job openings that require WebGL skills. These positions may include web developer, 3D artist, game developer, or UX designer roles.

Freelancing:

- Consider freelancing or offering your WebGL expertise on platforms like Upwork or Fiverr. Freelancing allows you to gain experience and build a client base.

Start Your Own Projects:

- If you have innovative ideas, don't hesitate to start your own WebGL projects. You can monetize them through crowdfunding, sponsorship, or online marketplaces.

Education and Training:

- Explore opportunities for teaching or providing workshops related to WebGL. Sharing your knowledge can be a fulfilling career path.

Building a WebGL portfolio is a rewarding journey that not only showcases your skills but also helps you grow as a developer. With a well-planned portfolio, effective presentation, online presence, networking, and career exploration, you can position yourself for success in the world of web graphics.

Chapter 16: Building a WebGL Portfolio

16.1. Planning Your Portfolio Projects

Before embarking on the journey of building a WebGL portfolio, it's crucial to have a clear plan in place. Your portfolio is a representation of your skills, creativity, and expertise in WebGL, and it can play a pivotal role in shaping your career or attracting clients if you're a freelancer. Here are some key considerations to keep in mind when planning your portfolio projects:

Define Your Goals:

The first step is to determine the primary purpose of your portfolio. Are you looking to land a job in the industry, showcase your work to potential clients, or simply establish your online presence as a WebGL developer? Clearly defining your goals will help you tailor your portfolio accordingly.

Showcase a Range:

It's essential to demonstrate your versatility as a WebGL developer. Try to include a diverse range of projects that showcase different aspects of your skills. This could include 3D games, interactive simulations, data visualizations, or creative experiments. Having a variety of projects can attract a wider audience and potential opportunities.

Quality Over Quantity:

While it's tempting to include as many projects as possible, it's often more effective to focus on quality rather than quantity. Having a few well-polished, outstanding projects is more likely to leave a lasting impression than a large number of mediocre ones. Concentrate on projects that truly highlight your skills and creativity.

Tell a Story:

Each project in your portfolio should tell a story. Start by explaining the problem or concept that your project addresses. Describe your approach and the techniques or technologies you used. Finally, share the impact or results of the project. Crafting a narrative around your work can engage visitors and help them understand your thought process.

Include Personal Projects:

Personal projects can set you apart and reveal your passion and initiative as a WebGL developer. They offer you the freedom to experiment and innovate without client constraints. Don't hesitate to include personal projects that you're proud of and that showcase your creativity.

Planning your portfolio projects strategically will not only make the portfolio-building process more efficient but also ensure that your portfolio effectively communicates your skills and achievements as a WebGL developer.

16.2. Effective Presentation of 3D Work

Creating a WebGL portfolio is not just about having great projects; it's also about presenting them effectively to leave a lasting impression on your visitors. Here are some strategies for presenting your 3D work effectively:

Clear Project Titles and Descriptions:

Each project in your portfolio should have a clear and concise title. The title should give visitors a hint of what the project is about. Follow the title with a brief description that provides context and a quick overview of the project's goals and outcomes. Make sure your descriptions are easy to understand, even for non-technical viewers.

High-Quality Visuals:

The visuals of your projects are critical. Use high-resolution images and screenshots to showcase your work. Consider including animated gifs or short video clips to give visitors a dynamic view of your projects in action. Ensure that the images accurately represent the quality and aesthetics of your 3D models and animations.

Interactive Demos:

Whenever possible, provide interactive demos of your projects. WebGL allows for real-time interactivity, so letting visitors explore your projects firsthand can be a powerful way to engage them. Embed interactive 3D views directly in your portfolio or provide links to dedicated project pages with live demos.

Code Samples and Technical Details:

For visitors interested in the technical aspects of your projects, include code samples or links to GitHub repositories. Explain your coding approach and any innovative techniques you used. Providing insights into your coding process can demonstrate your expertise and problem-solving abilities.

User Experience (UX):

Consider the user experience of your portfolio. Ensure that your portfolio website is easy to navigate and mobile-friendly. A well-designed user interface can enhance the overall impression visitors have of your work. Make it easy for visitors to contact you or find more information about your projects.

Testimonials and Recommendations:

If you've worked with clients or collaborators in the past, consider including testimonials or recommendations from them. Positive feedback from others can build trust and credibility, especially if you're looking to attract clients or employers.

Continuous Updates:

Your portfolio is not a static entity. Keep it up-to-date with your latest projects and improvements. Regularly review and refresh the content to ensure that it reflects your current skills and style as a WebGL developer.

Accessibility:

Ensure that your portfolio is accessible to all users, including those with disabilities. Follow web accessibility guidelines to make your content available to a wider audience.

In summary, presenting your 3D work effectively is just as important as the quality of the work itself. A well-organized, visually appealing, and informative portfolio can help you stand out in the competitive field of WebGL development.

16.3. Building an Online Presence

In the digital age, having an online presence is crucial for any professional, and WebGL developers are no exception. Your online presence serves as your virtual identity and can significantly impact your career opportunities and networking. Here are some key aspects of building and maintaining a strong online presence as a WebGL developer:

1. Portfolio Website:

Your portfolio website is your online showcase of your work. We discussed the importance of this in the previous section (16.2), but it's worth emphasizing. Your website should be well-designed, easy to navigate, and showcase your best projects prominently. Include a contact form or email address for potential clients or collaborators to reach out to you.

2. Social Media:

Leverage social media platforms to connect with the WebGL and 3D graphics community. Platforms like Twitter, LinkedIn, and Instagram can be great for sharing your work, networking with peers, and staying updated on industry trends. Use relevant hashtags to increase the discoverability of your posts.

3. Blogging and Content Creation:

Consider starting a blog or writing articles related to WebGL development. Sharing your knowledge and insights through blog posts or tutorials can position you as an expert in your field. It's also an excellent way to help others and contribute to the community.

4. Online Communities and Forums:

Join online communities and forums dedicated to WebGL and 3D graphics. Engage in discussions, seek advice, and share your expertise. Platforms like GitHub, Stack Overflow, and specialized WebGL forums can be valuable resources for learning and networking.

5. GitHub and Open Source Contributions:

If you're comfortable with open source development, contribute to relevant projects on GitHub. This not only showcases your coding skills but also allows you to collaborate with other developers. Being an active contributor to open source projects can enhance your credibility.

6. Online Courses and Webinars:

Consider creating online courses or webinars related to WebGL development. Platforms like Udemy, Coursera, or YouTube can help you reach a global audience. Offering educational content can establish you as a thought leader in the field.

7. Attend Virtual Conferences and Webinars:

While physical conferences are essential for networking, virtual conferences and webinars have become more prevalent. Participate in such events to learn from experts, connect with peers, and stay updated on industry advancements.

8. Personal Branding:

Define your personal brand as a WebGL developer. What sets you apart from others? Highlight your unique skills, style, and approach in your online presence. Consistency in branding across your website and social media profiles is crucial.

9. Networking:

Actively network with other WebGL developers, professionals in related fields, and potential clients. Attend online networking events, engage in discussions, and be open to collaborations. Networking can lead to exciting opportunities and partnerships.

10. Online Security and Privacy:

Ensure that you're mindful of online security and privacy. Protect sensitive information, use secure connections, and be cautious about sharing personal details online.

Remember that building an online presence takes time and effort. Consistency and authenticity are key. As you establish yourself in the WebGL community, your online presence can open doors to exciting projects, collaborations, and career growth opportunities.

16.4. Networking and Community Involvement

Networking and active community involvement are indispensable aspects of a successful WebGL developer's journey. By connecting with peers, experts, and enthusiasts in the field, you can learn, share knowledge, and discover exciting opportunities. Here are some strategies and tips for effective networking and community engagement:

1. Join WebGL Communities:

Start by joining online communities dedicated to WebGL and 3D graphics. Platforms like Reddit (r/WebGL), Stack Overflow, and specialized forums are great places to begin. These communities often host discussions, share resources, and provide solutions to common challenges.

2. Participate in Discussions:

Engage actively in discussions within these communities. Offer assistance to those in need, share your experiences, and ask questions when you encounter challenges. Meaningful interactions can help you establish yourself as a valuable member of the community.

3. Attend WebGL Meetups and Conferences:

Look for WebGL meetups, conferences, and webinars happening online or in your local area. Attending these events allows you to meet fellow developers, learn from experts, and stay updated on the latest trends and technologies in WebGL.

4. Collaborate on Projects:

Consider collaborating with other WebGL developers on projects or initiatives. Collaboration not only enhances your skills but also exposes you to different approaches and perspectives. It can lead to exciting opportunities and friendships.

5. Contribute to Open Source:

Open source projects are a fantastic way to give back to the community while improving your skills. Contribute to WebGL-related open source projects on platforms like GitHub. Your contributions can be anything from bug fixes to new features.

6. Create Educational Content:

Share your knowledge by creating educational content. Write blog posts, tutorials, or record video lessons related to WebGL development. Platforms like Medium, YouTube, and personal blogs are excellent channels for this.

7. Attend Web Development and Game Development Events:

Since WebGL often intersects with web development and game development, attending events related to these fields can broaden your network. You'll meet professionals with overlapping interests and expertise.

8. Engage on Social Media:

Leverage social media platforms to connect with fellow developers. Follow and interact with WebGL experts, join relevant groups, and share your own insights and projects. LinkedIn and Twitter are particularly useful for professional networking.

9. Offer Workshops or Webinars:

Consider organizing workshops or webinars on WebGL-related topics. These can attract an audience eager to learn, and you'll establish yourself as an authority in the subject matter.

10. Be Respectful and Professional:

Maintain professionalism and respect in all your interactions. Building a positive reputation in the community is essential for long-term success. Constructive criticism and helpful advice go a long way.

11. Stay Informed:

Stay updated with the latest developments in WebGL and related technologies. Knowledge is a valuable asset when networking and engaging in discussions. Subscribe to relevant blogs, newsletters, and news sources.

Networking and community involvement require dedication and genuine interest in the field. By actively participating in the WebGL community, you not only expand your knowledge but also form meaningful connections that can advance your career and open doors to exciting opportunities.

16.5. Finding Opportunities in WebGL Development

As a WebGL developer, you've acquired a valuable skill set that opens the door to numerous exciting career opportunities. Whether you're interested in freelance work, full-time employment, or starting your own WebGL-related business, there are several avenues to explore:

1. Game Development Studios:

Many game development studios incorporate WebGL into their projects. If you have a passion for game development, consider applying for positions as a WebGL developer in these studios. You may work on creating interactive 3D games, simulations, or gamified web applications.

2. Web Development Agencies:

Web development agencies often seek WebGL developers to enhance the interactivity and visual appeal of their clients' websites. You can find opportunities to work on various web projects, from product configurators to interactive marketing campaigns.

3. E-learning and EdTech:

The e-learning industry relies on WebGL for creating interactive educational content. Explore opportunities with e-learning companies or educational technology startups to develop engaging 3D educational materials.

4. Augmented and Virtual Reality:

As augmented reality (AR) and virtual reality (VR) technologies continue to advance, WebGL developers are in demand for creating AR and VR experiences on the web. Companies working in this space may require your expertise to build immersive web-based applications.

5. Creative Agencies:

Creative agencies often use WebGL to craft visually stunning experiences for their clients' marketing campaigns. You can work on projects that showcase your creativity and technical skills, such as interactive advertisements or branded web experiences.

6. Freelancing:

Freelancing as a WebGL developer gives you the flexibility to choose projects that align with your interests and skills. Platforms like Upwork, Freelancer, and Toptal connect freelancers with clients seeking WebGL expertise.

7. Start Your Own Projects:

Consider creating your own WebGL projects or games and monetizing them through platforms like itch.io or by offering premium versions. This entrepreneurial route allows you to build a portfolio while potentially generating income.

8. Education and Training:

Share your knowledge and expertise by becoming an instructor or course creator. Online learning platforms like Udemy, Coursera, and edX provide opportunities to teach WebGL and related topics to a global audience.

9. Research and Development:

Explore positions in research and development at companies or institutions that are pushing the boundaries of WebGL technology. Research roles may involve experimenting with new WebGL techniques or optimizing performance for specific use cases.

10. WebGL Consulting:

Offer consulting services to businesses looking to implement WebGL in their projects. You can provide guidance on best practices, code optimization, and project planning.

11. Software Development Companies:

Software development companies that create 3D modeling, simulation, or visualization software may require WebGL developers to integrate 3D capabilities into their products.

12. Cross-Disciplinary Roles:

WebGL's versatility allows you to work in cross-disciplinary roles that blend web development with other fields such as data visualization, art, design, or scientific research.

When seeking opportunities, build a strong online presence by showcasing your portfolio, contributing to the WebGL community, and networking with professionals in the industry. Stay updated on the latest WebGL trends and technologies to remain competitive in the job market. With determination and a passion for 3D web graphics, you can carve a rewarding career path in WebGL development.

Chapter 17: Advanced Topics in WebGL

17.1. Ray Tracing in WebGL

In the world of computer graphics, ray tracing is a rendering technique that simulates the way light interacts with objects in a scene. Unlike rasterization, which is the traditional rendering method used in WebGL, ray tracing offers more realistic lighting and shading effects. While ray tracing has historically been computationally intensive and reserved for offline rendering, recent advancements in GPU hardware and APIs like WebGL have brought real-time ray tracing within reach. In this section, we'll explore the fundamentals of ray tracing in WebGL and how to implement it for interactive 3D scenes.

Understanding Ray Tracing

Ray tracing involves simulating the path of light rays as they interact with objects in a 3D scene. It models the behavior of light by tracing rays from the camera's viewpoint into the scene. When a ray intersects an object, it calculates how the light interacts with the object's surface, including reflection, refraction, and shadowing effects.

Key components of ray tracing include:

- **Rays:** Rays originate from the camera and extend into the scene. Each ray represents a potential path that light can take.

- **Intersection Testing:** For each ray, the algorithm checks if it intersects any objects in the scene. This involves testing for intersections with primitives like spheres, triangles, or more complex geometric shapes.

- **Shading:** Once an intersection is found, the shading model calculates the color of the pixel at the intersection point. This includes evaluating lighting equations, material properties, and reflections.

- **Reflection and Refraction:** Rays can bounce off surfaces (reflection) or pass through transparent materials (refraction), simulating realistic behaviors of light.

- **Shadows:** Ray tracing determines whether a point is in shadow by tracing rays toward light sources to check for occlusions.

WebGL and Ray Tracing

Implementing ray tracing in WebGL involves significant challenges due to the limitations of JavaScript and the WebGL API. Real-time ray tracing can be computationally demanding, and optimizing performance is crucial. Here are some key considerations:

- **Acceleration Structures:** To speed up intersection testing, WebGL ray tracing often uses acceleration structures like bounding volume hierarchies (BVH) or spatial partitioning.

- **Shading and Materials:** WebGL shaders must be designed to handle complex shading models and material properties to achieve realistic lighting effects.

- **Performance Optimization:** Efficient algorithms and data structures are essential to maintain real-time frame rates. WebGL's parallel processing capabilities are leveraged to accelerate ray tracing operations.

- **GPU Compute:** Modern GPUs offer support for general-purpose computing, enabling the use of shaders for ray tracing calculations.

- **Fallbacks:** WebGL ray tracers may provide fallbacks for devices that do not support real-time ray tracing, such as using traditional rasterization for less capable hardware.

In this section, we'll delve into the principles of ray tracing and explore WebGL-specific techniques for implementing it. We'll cover intersection testing, shading, reflections, and optimizations to help you get started with real-time ray tracing in WebGL.

17.2. Implementing Realistic Water Effects

Simulating realistic water in WebGL is a complex and fascinating challenge. Water surfaces are dynamic, reflective, and refractive, which makes them visually appealing in 3D scenes. In this section, we'll explore various techniques to implement realistic water effects in WebGL.

1. Reflection and Refraction

One of the essential aspects of water rendering is achieving reflection and refraction. Reflection involves rendering the environment as seen from the water's surface, while refraction involves bending light as it passes through the water surface. Achieving this effect requires rendering the scene twice: once from the viewpoint above the water surface (reflection) and once from the viewpoint below the water surface (refraction). You can then blend these two images to create a realistic water appearance.

2. Normal Mapping

Normal mapping is a technique used to simulate fine surface details on 3D models without increasing the model's polygon count. It works by encoding surface normals in a texture, allowing you to simulate intricate water ripples and waves on the water surface. Implementing normal mapping in WebGL requires shaders that use the normal map texture to perturb normals during rendering, creating the illusion of depth and detail.

3. Fresnel Effect

The Fresnel effect is the phenomenon where the reflectance of a material varies with the viewing angle. It is particularly noticeable on water surfaces, where the reflection is more prominent when viewed at shallow angles and diminishes as the angle approaches 90 degrees (viewing straight down). Implementing the Fresnel effect in WebGL shaders can enhance the realism of water materials.

4. Wave Simulation

Realistic water requires the simulation of waves and ripples. Various techniques, such as Gerstner waves or Fast Fourier Transform (FFT) waves, can be used to simulate water surface displacement. These techniques allow you to create dynamic and visually pleasing water animations. WebGL shaders can be employed to apply these displacement maps to the water surface vertices.

5. Specular Highlights

Specular highlights are the bright, reflective spots that appear on water surfaces when illuminated by a light source. Implementing specular highlights in WebGL shaders involves calculating the reflection vector based on the light direction and surface normal.

By modulating the intensity of these highlights, you can achieve a convincing water surface appearance.

6. Post-processing Effects

Post-processing effects, such as bloom and depth of field, can enhance the visual quality of water rendering. Bloom can be used to simulate the scattering of light by water droplets in the air, creating a dreamy and visually appealing look. Depth of field can be applied to the scene to simulate the blurring effect that occurs when looking through water.

7. Performance Considerations

Implementing realistic water effects in WebGL can be computationally intensive, especially when simulating waves and applying multiple shaders. To maintain good performance, consider using techniques like level of detail (LOD) for distant water surfaces and optimizing shaders for parallel execution on the GPU.

In conclusion, achieving realistic water effects in WebGL involves a combination of reflection, refraction, normal mapping, Fresnel effects, wave simulation, specular highlights, and post-processing effects. By carefully implementing these techniques and optimizing for performance, you can create visually stunning water surfaces in your 3D scenes.

17.3. Advanced Texturing Techniques

Texturing plays a crucial role in 3D graphics, as it adds detail, realism, and depth to objects and scenes. In this section, we'll explore advanced texturing techniques in WebGL that go beyond basic texture mapping.

1. Cube Mapping

Cube mapping is a technique used to simulate reflections and environment mapping. It involves using six separate textures (one for each face of a cube) to represent the environment around an object. Cube maps are often used for rendering reflective surfaces like water, glass, and metal. In WebGL, you can implement cube mapping by creating six textures and sampling them based on the reflection vector in your fragment shader.

```
// Example WebGL cube mapping in a fragment shader

uniform samplerCube cubeMap;

varying vec3 reflectionVector;

void main() {

gl_FragColor = textureCube(cubeMap, reflectionVector);

}
```

2. Parallax Mapping

Parallax mapping is a technique used to simulate depth and relief on 3D surfaces without adding additional geometry. It achieves this by perturbing the texture coordinates based on a height map. As the view angle changes, the illusion of depth is created, enhancing the realism of surfaces. Implementing parallax mapping in WebGL requires shaders that sample a height map and adjust texture coordinates accordingly.

```
// Example WebGL parallax mapping in a vertex shader

attribute vec3 vertexPosition;

attribute vec2 vertexUV;
```

```
uniform sampler2D heightMap;

varying vec2 texCoord;

void main() {

// Calculate displaced texture coordinates based on the height map

vec2 displacedTexCoord = calculateDisplacement(vertexUV,
heightMap);

// Pass the displaced coordinates to the fragment shader

texCoord = displacedTexCoord;

// Other vertex shader code...

}
```

3. Anisotropic Filtering

Anisotropic filtering is a texture filtering technique that improves the quality of textures when viewed at oblique angles. It helps reduce the blurring and distortion of textures on surfaces that are not parallel to the camera. To enable anisotropic filtering in WebGL, you can set the appropriate texture filtering parameters when loading textures.

```
// Example enabling anisotropic filtering in WebGL

const texture = gl.createTexture();

gl.bindTexture(gl.TEXTURE_2D, texture);

gl.texParameteri(gl.TEXTURE_2D,
gl.TEXTURE_MIN_FILTER,
gl.LINEAR_MIPMAP_LINEAR);
```

gl.texParameteri(gl.TEXTURE_2D, gl.TEXTURE_MAG_FILTER, gl.LINEAR);

gl.texParameterf(gl.TEXTURE_2D, gl.TEXTURE_MAX_ANISOTROPY_EXT, maxAnisotropy);

4. Texture Atlases

Texture atlases are a space-efficient way to store multiple textures in a single image. They are commonly used for optimizing games and applications by reducing the number of texture switches. In WebGL, you can implement texture atlases by adjusting texture coordinates in your shaders to select the desired texture region from the atlas.

```
// Example WebGL texture atlas in a fragment shader

uniform sampler2D atlasTexture;

varying vec2 texCoord;

void main() {

// Calculate texture coordinates within the atlas

vec2 atlasCoord = calculateAtlasCoord(texCoord);

// Sample from the atlas

gl_FragColor = texture2D(atlasTexture, atlasCoord);

}
```

5. Procedural Textures

Procedural textures are generated algorithmically rather than being based on images. They can be used to create a wide range of effects, from wood grain and marble to clouds and fire. In WebGL, you can implement procedural textures by defining functions in your shaders to generate texture values based on mathematical equations or noise functions.

```
// Example WebGL procedural texture in a fragment shader

varying vec2 texCoord;

void main() {

// Generate procedural texture value based on texCoord

vec3 color = generateProceduralTexture(texCoord);

// Assign the color to the fragment

gl_FragColor = vec4(color, 1.0);

}
```

These advanced texturing techniques allow you to create more realistic and visually appealing 3D scenes in WebGL. Experimenting with these techniques and combining them can result in stunning visual effects and improved realism in your web-based 3D applications.

17.4. Working with High Dynamic Range Imaging

High Dynamic Range (HDR) imaging is a technique that captures and displays a wider range of luminance values than standard images. HDR images store pixel values with higher precision, allowing for a more accurate representation of real-world lighting conditions. In WebGL, working with HDR imaging can greatly enhance the visual quality of your 3D scenes and create realistic lighting effects.

HDR Textures

To work with HDR images in WebGL, you need HDR textures. These textures use formats that store high-precision color values. WebGL supports various HDR texture formats, such as RGBA16F and RGBA32F, which represent color values using floating-point numbers. When loading HDR textures, ensure that you specify the appropriate texture format and internal format to match the HDR data.

```
// Example WebGL code for loading an HDR texture

const texture = gl.createTexture();

gl.bindTexture(gl.TEXTURE_2D, texture);

// Set texture parameters for HDR format

gl.texImage2D(gl.TEXTURE_2D, 0, gl.RGBA16F, gl.RGBA, gl.FLOAT, hdrImageData);
```

HDR Rendering

When rendering with HDR textures, you must adjust your shaders and rendering pipeline to accommodate the extended color range. Your fragment shaders should be capable of performing arithmetic operations with high-precision floating-point values. Additionally, you may need to apply tonemapping techniques to convert HDR values into a suitable range for display on standard monitors.

```
// Example WebGL fragment shader for HDR rendering with tonemapping

uniform sampler2D hdrTexture;

varying vec2 texCoord;
```

```
void main() {

// Sample HDR pixel value

vec4 hdrColor = texture2D(hdrTexture, texCoord);

// Apply tonemapping to convert HDR to LDR

vec3 ldrColor = tonemap(hdrColor.rgb);

// Assign the result to the fragment

gl_FragColor = vec4(ldrColor, 1.0);

}
```

HDR Lighting

Using HDR imaging in your WebGL projects allows you to simulate more realistic lighting conditions. HDR light sources can have a wider range of intensities, providing greater flexibility for creating visually stunning scenes. To incorporate HDR lighting, you can define light sources with high-intensity values and ensure that your shaders support HDR color calculations.

```
// Example WebGL shader code for HDR lighting

uniform vec3 hdrLightColor; // HDR light color

uniform float hdrLightIntensity; // HDR light intensity

void main() {

// Calculate HDR lighting contribution

vec3 hdrLight = hdrLightColor * hdrLightIntensity;

// Other lighting calculations...
```

```
// Combine HDR lighting with other contributions

vec3 finalColor = diffuseColor * hdrLight;

// Assign the result to the fragment

gl_FragColor = vec4(finalColor, 1.0);

}
```

Post-Processing Effects

HDR rendering can be combined with post-processing effects to enhance the visual quality of your WebGL scenes. Effects like bloom, glare, and lens flares are particularly effective when working with HDR imagery. These effects take advantage of the extended dynamic range to create visually appealing and realistic renderings.

```
// Example WebGL post-processing effect for bloom

uniform sampler2D hdrTexture;

varying vec2 texCoord;

void main() {

// Sample the HDR texture

vec3 hdrColor = texture2D(hdrTexture, texCoord).rgb;

// Apply bloom effect...

// Assign the result to the fragment

gl_FragColor = vec4(bloomColor, 1.0);

}
```

Working with high dynamic range imaging in WebGL opens up a wide range of possibilities for creating visually stunning and realistic 3D graphics. By incorporating HDR textures, rendering techniques, lighting, and post-processing effects, you can achieve lifelike visuals that captivate your audience and provide a more immersive web-based experience.

17.5. Procedural Generation in WebGL

Procedural generation is a technique widely used in game development and computer graphics to create content algorithmically rather than manually designing it. In WebGL, procedural generation can be a powerful tool for generating terrain, textures, and even entire worlds. This section explores the concept of procedural generation in WebGL and provides insights into its implementation.

What Is Procedural Generation?

Procedural generation refers to the process of creating content using algorithms or mathematical functions. Instead of handcrafting every aspect of a scene, developers define rules and algorithms that generate content dynamically. This approach has several advantages, including the ability to create vast and diverse worlds, reduce asset storage requirements, and add variety to gameplay experiences.

Procedural Terrain Generation

One common application of procedural generation in WebGL is terrain generation. You can use algorithms to create realistic landscapes with mountains, valleys, rivers, and more. Popular techniques for procedural terrain generation include Perlin noise, Voronoi diagrams, and diamond-square algorithms.

Here's a simplified example of using Perlin noise to generate a terrain heightmap in WebGL:

```
// Example WebGL code for terrain generation using Perlin noise

const width = 512;

const height = 512;

const scale = 0.1;

const terrain = new Float32Array(width * height);

for (let y = 0; y < height; y++) {

for (let x = 0; x < width; x++) {

const nx = x / width - 0.5;

const ny = y / height - 0.5;

const elevation = noise(nx * scale, ny * scale);

terrain[y * width + x] = elevation;

}

}
```

Procedural Texture Generation

In addition to terrain, procedural generation can be used to create textures dynamically. Procedural textures can simulate natural patterns like wood, marble, or clouds, and they can be generated in real-time to adapt to different scenarios.

Here's a simplified example of generating a procedural wood texture in WebGL:

```
// Example WebGL code for procedural wood texture generation
const width = 512;
const height = 512;
const woodTexture = new Uint8Array(width * height * 4);
for (let y = 0; y < height; y++) {
for (let x = 0; x < width; x++) {
const r = Math.sin(x / width * Math.PI * 10);
const g = Math.sin(y / height * Math.PI * 10);
const b = (r + g) / 2;
const a = 255;
const index = (y * width + x) * 4;
woodTexture[index] = r * 255;
woodTexture[index + 1] = g * 255;
woodTexture[index + 2] = b * 255;
woodTexture[index + 3] = a;
}
}
```

Applications of Procedural Generation

Procedural generation has a wide range of applications in WebGL, including game development, virtual worlds, and simulations. It allows developers to create large and diverse environments efficiently, saving both time and storage space. Procedurally generated content can also adapt to user interactions or specific gameplay scenarios, ensuring a dynamic and engaging experience.

When using procedural generation in WebGL, it's essential to balance creativity and performance. Complex procedural algorithms can be computationally intensive, so optimization and efficient rendering techniques are crucial for delivering smooth and interactive 3D experiences.

In conclusion, procedural generation in WebGL offers exciting opportunities to create dynamic and diverse content. Whether you're generating terrain, textures, or entire worlds, understanding the principles of procedural generation can elevate your WebGL projects and provide unique and engaging experiences for users.

18.1. Common WebGL Pitfalls and Solutions

WebGL is a powerful technology for creating 3D graphics on the web, but like any technology, it comes with its set of challenges and common pitfalls. In this section, we will explore some of the common issues developers face when working with WebGL and provide solutions to overcome them.

1. Cross-Browser Compatibility

Pitfall: WebGL support varies across different web browsers and devices. Your application may work perfectly in one browser but encounter issues in another.

Solution: To ensure cross-browser compatibility, always test your WebGL application in multiple browsers, including Google Chrome, Mozilla Firefox, Safari, and Microsoft Edge. Use a library like Three.js, which provides an abstraction layer that handles browser differences for you.

2. Shader Errors

Pitfall: Writing and debugging shaders can be challenging. Small errors in your GLSL code can lead to unexpected rendering issues or even crashes.

Solution: Use development tools like the WebGL Inspector and Shader Editor to debug your shaders. Additionally, check your shader code for common mistakes such as uninitialized variables, division by zero, or incorrect variable types.

3. Resource Loading

Pitfall: Loading 3D models, textures, and other assets asynchronously can be error-prone, leading to missing or improperly loaded resources.

Solution: Implement a robust resource loading system that handles errors gracefully. Libraries like Ammo.js and GLTFLoader can help simplify resource loading tasks.

4. Memory Management

Pitfall: WebGL applications can consume a significant amount of memory, especially when dealing with large textures or complex 3D scenes.

Solution: Efficiently manage memory by releasing unused resources and textures when they are no longer needed. Implement a garbage collection system to free up memory occupied by unused WebGL objects.

5. Performance Optimization

Pitfall: WebGL performance can be a bottleneck, particularly on mobile devices or older hardware.

Solution: Profile your application using tools like Chrome DevTools' Performance tab or Mozilla's PerfHUD to identify performance bottlenecks. Optimize your rendering code, minimize texture size, and use techniques like level-of-detail (LOD) to improve performance.

6. Security Considerations

Pitfall: WebGL applications can potentially expose security vulnerabilities if not properly secured.

Solution: Follow security best practices, such as avoiding WebGL extensions that may expose sensitive information, and sanitizing user inputs to prevent WebGL-based attacks.

7. Mobile Optimization

Pitfall: Porting WebGL applications to mobile devices can be challenging due to differences in performance and input methods.

Solution: Adapt your WebGL application for mobile by optimizing shaders, using touch-friendly controls, and testing on various mobile devices. Consider using libraries like React 360 for building VR experiences on mobile.

8. WebAssembly Integration

Pitfall: WebAssembly can enhance WebGL performance, but integrating it can be complex.

Solution: Learn how to integrate WebAssembly modules into your WebGL applications to take advantage of its performance benefits. Tools like Emscripten can simplify the process of compiling C/C++ code to WebAssembly.

9. Keeping Up-to-Date

Pitfall: WebGL is an evolving technology, and staying up-to-date with the latest features and best practices can be challenging.

Solution: Regularly follow updates and documentation from the WebGL community, attend WebGL-related conferences, and engage with the developer community to stay informed about the latest advancements and best practices.

In conclusion, WebGL is a versatile technology for creating 3D web applications, but it comes with its share of challenges. By being aware of common pitfalls and implementing the suggested solutions, you can create more robust and efficient WebGL applications that work across various browsers and devices.

18.2. Best Practices for Code Organization

When working on WebGL projects, maintaining a well-organized codebase is crucial for readability, maintainability, and collaboration with other developers. In this section, we'll explore best practices for organizing your WebGL code effectively.

1. Modularization

Modularization is a fundamental principle in code organization. Divide your WebGL code into separate modules or files, each responsible for a specific aspect of your application. For example, you can have separate modules for shaders, 3D models, textures, and user interface components. This approach simplifies code maintenance and makes it easier to collaborate with other developers.

```
// Example of modularization

import { initWebGL, createShaderProgram, loadTexture } from './webgl-utils.js';

import { createModel, renderModel } from './model-utils.js';

const gl = initWebGL('canvas');

const program = createShaderProgram(gl, 'vertex-shader', 'fragment-shader');

const texture = loadTexture(gl, 'texture.png');

const model = createModel(gl, program, texture);

// ...

renderModel(gl, model);
```

2. Shader Separation

Keep your vertex and fragment shaders separate from your JavaScript code. Store them in separate files with appropriate file extensions (e.g., .vert for vertex shaders and .frag for fragment shaders). This separation enhances readability and simplifies shader debugging and updates.

```
// Example of shader separation (vertex shader)

// vertex-shader.vert

attribute vec4 a_position;

attribute vec2 a_texcoord;
```

```
varying vec2 v_texcoord;

void main() {

gl_Position = a_position;

v_texcoord = a_texcoord;

}
```

3. Encapsulation

Encapsulate related WebGL functionality into classes or objects. For instance, create a WebGLRenderer class to handle rendering tasks, a TextureManager class to manage textures, and a ShaderProgram class to manage shader programs. This encapsulation promotes clean and maintainable code.

```
// Example of encapsulation (WebGLRenderer class)

class WebGLRenderer {

constructor(canvas) {

this.gl = initWebGL(canvas);

}

render(model) {

// Rendering logic here

}

// Other WebGL-related methods

}
```

4. Consistent Naming Conventions

Follow consistent naming conventions for variables, functions, and classes. Use descriptive and meaningful names that convey the purpose and usage of each entity. Consistency in naming promotes code readability and reduces confusion.

```
// Example of consistent naming conventions

function loadTexture(gl, url) {

// ...

}

class ShaderProgram {

constructor(gl, vertexShaderSource, fragmentShaderSource) {

// ...

}

// ...

}
```

5. Documentation and Comments

Document your code thoroughly. Use comments to explain complex logic, important considerations, and the purpose of functions and classes. Good documentation makes it easier for both you and other developers to understand and maintain the codebase.

```
// Example of code documentation

/**
```

```
* Loads a texture from the given URL.

* @param {WebGLRenderingContext} gl - The WebGL context.

* @param {string} url - The URL of the texture image.

* @returns {WebGLTexture} - The loaded texture.

*/

function loadTexture(gl, url) {

// ...

}
```

6. Version Control

Use version control systems like Git to track changes to your codebase. Version control helps you collaborate with other developers, roll back to previous states, and maintain a history of your project's development.

```
# Example Git commands

git init

git add .

git commit -m "Initial commit"

git push origin master
```

7. Build Tools

Consider using build tools like Webpack or Parcel to bundle and optimize your WebGL application for production. These tools can help manage dependencies, minify code, and reduce the size of your final application, improving load times and performance.

```
// Example of Webpack configuration
module.exports = {
entry: './src/main.js',
output: {
filename: 'bundle.js',
path: path.resolve(__dirname, 'dist'),
},
// ...
};
```

By following these best practices for code organization, you can maintain a clean and well-structured WebGL codebase that is easier to work with, collaborate on, and extend as your project evolves.

18.3. Ensuring Cross-Browser Compatibility

When developing WebGL applications, ensuring cross-browser compatibility is essential to reach a broader audience. Different web browsers may have varying levels of support for WebGL and may require specific considerations. In this section, we'll explore how to ensure that your WebGL projects work smoothly across multiple browsers.

1. Browser Feature Detection

One of the first steps in achieving cross-browser compatibility is to perform browser feature detection rather than relying on user agent strings. Feature detection allows you to check if a particular WebGL feature or API is supported by the user's browser before attempting to use it. This approach ensures that your application gracefully degrades or provides alternative functionality when WebGL is not supported.

```
// Example of WebGL feature detection

if (window.WebGLRenderingContext) {

const canvas = document.getElementById('canvas');

const gl = canvas.getContext('webgl');

if (!gl) {

// WebGL is not supported

// Provide fallback content or display an error message

} else {

// WebGL is supported, continue with your WebGL code

}

} else {

// WebGL is not supported

// Provide fallback content or display an error message

}
```

2. Polyfills and Shims

In cases where certain WebGL features or APIs are not available in older browsers, you can use polyfills or shims to provide compatibility. Polyfills are JavaScript libraries that implement missing features, allowing your code to run consistently across browsers.

For example, you can use the webgl-legacy polyfill to add WebGL 1.0 support to browsers that only support WebGL 2.0.

```
// Example of using a WebGL polyfill

if (window.WebGLRenderingContext) {

const canvas = document.getElementById('canvas');

const gl = canvas.getContext('webgl') ||
canvas.getContext('experimental-webgl');

if (!gl) {

// Try using a WebGL 1.0 polyfill

const gl1 = canvas.getContext('webgl-legacy');

if (!gl1) {

// WebGL is not supported

// Provide fallback content or display an error message

} else {

// WebGL 1.0 is supported with polyfill, continue with your WebGL
code

}
```

```
} else {
// WebGL 2.0 is supported, continue with your WebGL code
}
} else {
// WebGL is not supported
// Provide fallback content or display an error message
}
```

3. Browser-Specific Workarounds

Sometimes, you may encounter specific issues or limitations in certain browsers. In such cases, it may be necessary to implement browser-specific workarounds or fixes. These workarounds can involve adjusting shader code, modifying rendering techniques, or using alternative approaches to achieve the desired functionality.

```
// Example of a browser-specific workaround
if (isSafariBrowser()) {
// Apply a workaround for Safari
// Modify shader code or rendering logic if necessary
} else if (isFirefoxBrowser()) {
// Apply a workaround for Firefox
// Adjust rendering techniques or implement specific fixes
} else {
// No browser-specific workaround needed
```

```
// Continue with standard WebGL code

}
```

4. Testing Across Browsers

To ensure cross-browser compatibility, regularly test your WebGL application on different browsers and their various versions. Consider using browser testing tools or services to automate the testing process and identify any issues early in the development cycle.

By following these practices, you can create WebGL applications that work seamlessly across a wide range of web browsers, providing a consistent and enjoyable experience for all users, regardless of their browser choice.

18.4. Security Considerations in WebGL

WebGL offers powerful capabilities for creating interactive 3D graphics on the web, but it also introduces potential security risks that developers need to be aware of. In this section, we'll explore some key security considerations when working with WebGL to ensure the safety of both your application and its users.

1. Cross-Origin Resource Sharing (CORS)

One of the primary security mechanisms in web browsers is the Same-Origin Policy, which restricts web pages from making requests to domains other than the one that served the web page. When loading external resources, such as textures or models, from different origins in a WebGL application, you need to handle Cross-Origin Resource Sharing (CORS) correctly.

To avoid security issues, ensure that the external resources you load have appropriate CORS headers set on the server. You can also use proxy servers or CDNs that support CORS to fetch resources securely.

2. Shader Injection Attacks

WebGL shaders are written in GLSL (OpenGL Shading Language), and they execute on the user's GPU. However, poorly sanitized or maliciously crafted shader code can lead to shader injection attacks. It's crucial to validate and sanitize any shader code that is dynamically generated or provided by users.

```
// Example of shader code injection prevention

const userProvidedCode = getUserProvidedShaderCode();

const sanitizedCode = sanitizeShaderCode(userProvidedCode);

if (isShaderCodeSafe(sanitizedCode)) {

// Use the sanitized shader code

const shader = createShader(gl, sanitizedCode);

// ...

} else {

// Handle or reject unsafe shader code

showSecurityWarning();

}
```

3. WebGL Debugging and Security Tools

Several debugging and security tools are available to help identify potential security vulnerabilities in WebGL applications. Tools like WebGL Inspector and Spector.js can assist in analyzing WebGL calls, shaders, and textures. They can also help you detect any unintended resource leaks or performance bottlenecks.

4. Controlling Access to Sensitive Data

If your WebGL application handles sensitive data, such as user-generated content, ensure that access to this data is tightly controlled. Implement proper authentication and authorization mechanisms to prevent unauthorized users from accessing or manipulating sensitive information.

5. WebGL Sandbox

Some browsers offer the option to run WebGL content in a sandboxed environment, which restricts certain WebGL features and capabilities. While this can enhance security, it may also limit the functionality of your application. Consider the trade-offs and user experience when enabling or disabling WebGL sandboxing.

6. Regular Updates

Keep your WebGL libraries and dependencies up to date. WebGL libraries often release updates to address security vulnerabilities and improve performance. Staying current with updates helps protect your application from known security issues.

7. Security Audits

Consider conducting security audits and penetration testing on your WebGL application to identify and address potential vulnerabilities. Security experts can help you assess your application's security posture and provide recommendations for improvement.

By proactively addressing these security considerations, you can create WebGL applications that not only deliver impressive 3D experiences but also prioritize the safety and privacy of your users.

18.5. Keeping Up-to-Date with WebGL Developments

WebGL is a dynamic and evolving technology, and it's essential for developers to stay informed about the latest developments, standards, and best practices. In this section, we'll explore why keeping up-to-date with WebGL is crucial and provide some tips for staying current.

1. Evolving Standards

WebGL is based on the OpenGL ES standard, and as such, it evolves alongside changes in the OpenGL standard. New versions of WebGL may introduce performance improvements, bug fixes, and additional features. Staying updated allows you to take advantage of these improvements and ensure your applications remain compatible with modern browsers.

2. Browser Updates

Web browsers are continually being updated and improved. These updates may introduce changes in how WebGL is implemented and supported. To ensure your WebGL applications work smoothly across various browsers, it's crucial to test and adapt your code as needed when new browser versions are released.

3. Emerging Technologies

The field of web graphics is continually evolving, and new technologies and APIs may complement or influence WebGL. For example, WebGPU is an emerging standard designed to provide lower-level access to GPU hardware and may become relevant for high-performance graphics applications. Keeping an eye on emerging technologies can help you make informed decisions about the future of your WebGL projects.

4. Community Engagement

Engaging with the WebGL developer community can be an excellent way to stay informed. Participating in online forums, attending web graphics conferences, and following WebGL-related blogs and social media accounts can help you learn from others, share knowledge, and stay updated on industry trends.

5. Documentation and Tutorials

WebGL documentation and tutorials are valuable resources for developers. They can help you understand new features, troubleshoot issues, and learn best practices. Regularly reviewing official documentation and exploring tutorials from reputable sources can enhance your skills and keep you up-to-date.

6. Experimentation and Exploration

WebGL development often involves experimentation and exploration. Don't hesitate to try out new techniques, libraries, or frameworks. Building small prototype projects can help you gain hands-on experience with the latest WebGL features and capabilities.

7. Feedback and Collaboration

Collaborating with other developers and seeking feedback on your WebGL projects can provide fresh insights and perspectives. It can also lead to valuable discussions about new techniques or approaches. Open source projects and online communities are great places to collaborate and learn from others.

In conclusion, staying up-to-date with WebGL developments is essential for creating high-quality 3D graphics applications that remain compatible and performant across various platforms and browsers. By embracing new standards, staying engaged with the community, and continually exploring and learning, you can ensure your WebGL skills remain sharp and your projects remain on the cutting edge of web graphics technology.

19.1. Joining the WebGL Developer Community

Joining the WebGL developer community is a fantastic way to enhance your skills, collaborate with like-minded individuals, and stay updated on the latest trends and techniques in the field of 3D web graphics. In this section, we'll explore the benefits of becoming part of the WebGL community and provide tips on how to get involved.

1. Benefits of Community Participation

Participating in the WebGL community offers numerous advantages:

- **Learning Opportunities**: Engaging with experienced developers allows you to learn from their expertise. You can gain insights into best practices, discover new techniques, and receive feedback on your work.

- **Networking**: Building connections within the community can open doors to collaborations, job opportunities, and knowledge sharing. Networking with professionals in the field can be instrumental in your career.

- **Problem Solving**: When you encounter challenges or roadblocks in your projects, the community can provide solutions and guidance. Many developers are willing to help troubleshoot issues and provide valuable advice.

- **Exposure**: Sharing your WebGL projects and contributions with the community can give your work greater visibility. Others can benefit from your insights, and you may receive recognition for your contributions.

2. Getting Involved

Here's how you can get started and become an active member of the WebGL developer community:

a. Online Forums and Communities

There are several online forums and communities dedicated to WebGL and 3D web graphics. These platforms are great places to ask questions, seek help, and share your knowledge. Some popular options include:

- **Khronos WebGL Forum**: Khronos Group's official forum for WebGL discussions.

- **Stack Overflow**: Stack Overflow is a valuable resource for asking technical questions related to WebGL.

- **GitHub**: Explore WebGL-related projects and contribute to open source development on GitHub.

b. Social Media

Platforms like Twitter, Reddit, and LinkedIn host WebGL communities and discussions. Follow relevant hashtags, join WebGL-related groups, and connect with professionals in the field.

c. WebGL Conferences and Meetups

Attending WebGL conferences and meetups can be a fantastic way to network and learn from experts. Look for events in your region or consider attending online conferences and webinars.

d. Open Source Contributions

Contributing to open source WebGL projects is an excellent way to showcase your skills and collaborate with others. Explore projects on GitHub and offer your help in fixing issues or adding new features.

3. Etiquette and Collaboration

When participating in the WebGL community, it's essential to maintain a positive and collaborative attitude. Follow these guidelines:

- **Respect Others**: Treat fellow developers with respect and courtesy, even if you disagree with their opinions. Constructive criticism is encouraged, but avoid personal attacks.

- **Share Knowledge**: Don't hesitate to share your knowledge and experiences. Helping others is an essential part of community engagement.

- **Ask Thoughtful Questions**: When seeking help, provide as much context as possible and ask clear, well-structured questions. This makes it easier for others to assist you.

- **Contribute Back**: If you benefit from open source projects, consider giving back by contributing code, documentation, or bug reports.

- **Stay Informed**: Keep up-to-date with community discussions, news, and events. Active participation requires ongoing engagement.

In summary, joining the WebGL developer community can be immensely rewarding both personally and professionally. It provides opportunities for learning, networking, and collaboration that can significantly enhance your skills and contribute to the growth of the field. So, don't hesitate to become an active member of this vibrant community.

19.2. Essential Online Resources and Forums

In addition to actively participating in the WebGL developer community, it's crucial to be aware of essential online resources and forums that can aid in your journey to mastering WebGL. These resources provide valuable documentation, tutorials, code samples, and more to help you excel in 3D web graphics.

1. Khronos Group

The Khronos Group is the organization behind WebGL, and their website is a treasure trove of information. You can find the official WebGL specification, documentation, and updates on the latest developments. Khronos also hosts the official WebGL forum, where developers discuss topics related to WebGL implementation, best practices, and troubleshooting.

2. MDN Web Docs

MDN Web Docs is an excellent resource provided by Mozilla. It offers comprehensive documentation on the WebGL API, including detailed explanations of functions, objects, and concepts. MDN also provides interactive examples and tutorials to help you grasp WebGL concepts effectively.

3. Stack Overflow

Stack Overflow is a popular platform for asking and answering technical questions. The WebGL tag on Stack Overflow is a valuable resource for troubleshooting issues and finding solutions to common problems. You can also contribute by answering questions and sharing your knowledge with the community.

4. GitHub

GitHub is home to numerous WebGL-related projects and libraries. By exploring repositories and reading source code, you can gain insights into WebGL implementation and best practices. You can also contribute to open source projects or create your WebGL projects on GitHub for collaboration and version control.

5. Three.js Documentation

Three.js[6] is a popular JavaScript library for creating 3D graphics with WebGL. Their website provides extensive documentation, including API reference, tutorials, and examples. If you plan to work with Three.js, this resource is indispensable for understanding the library's capabilities and how to use them effectively.

---

6. https://threejs.org/

6. WebGL Blogs and Tutorials

Many developers and organizations maintain blogs and tutorials dedicated to WebGL. These resources often include in-depth explanations, code samples, and real-world examples. Websites like LearningWebGL[7] and WebGL Academy[8] offer tutorials suitable for beginners and intermediate developers.

7. WebGL Books

There are several books available that cover WebGL in detail. These books provide structured learning paths, practical examples, and advanced techniques. Some notable titles include "WebGL Programming Guide" by Matsuda and Lea and "Interactive Computer Graphics: A Top-Down Approach with WebGL" by Edward Angel and Dave Shreiner.

8. Community Forums and Social Media

Apart from the official Khronos Group forum, there are other community-driven forums and discussions related to WebGL. Websites like WebGL Developer[9] and gamedev.stackexchange host discussions on WebGL topics. Additionally, following relevant hashtags and accounts on social media platforms like Twitter and LinkedIn can keep you updated on the latest news and trends in WebGL development.

In conclusion, these essential online resources and forums are valuable companions on your WebGL journey. Whether you're looking for official documentation, interactive tutorials, or community discussions, these sources offer a wealth of knowledge

---

7. http://learningwebgl.com/

8. https://www.webglacademy.com/

9. http://webgldeveloper.com/

to help you become a proficient WebGL developer. Remember to explore and leverage these resources to enhance your skills and stay up-to-date with the latest advancements in 3D web graphics.

19.3. Recommended Books and Tutorials

In your quest to become a proficient WebGL developer, turning to books and tutorials can be an excellent way to gain in-depth knowledge, discover practical examples, and learn from experts in the field. Here, we'll explore some recommended books and tutorials that cover various aspects of WebGL.

WebGL Books

1. "WebGL Programming Guide" by Matsuda and Lea

This book is a comprehensive guide to WebGL, offering a structured approach to understanding its core concepts and techniques. It covers everything from basic graphics programming to more advanced topics like shaders, texturing, and interactive 3D graphics. With numerous examples and exercises, it's suitable for both beginners and experienced developers.

2. "Interactive Computer Graphics: A Top-Down Approach with WebGL" by Edward Angel and Dave Shreiner

This book takes a top-down approach to computer graphics, using WebGL to illustrate concepts. It covers fundamental graphics principles, WebGL programming, and includes practical exercises and projects. The book provides a strong foundation for understanding the theory behind computer graphics.

3. "OpenGL Programming for the X Window System" by Mark J. Kilgard

While not exclusively focused on WebGL, this classic book delves into OpenGL, the underlying graphics API for WebGL. It's a valuable resource for those interested in understanding the core concepts and principles that WebGL builds upon. The book is well-regarded for its clarity and depth.

Online Tutorials

4. MDN Web Docs - WebGL

Mozilla's MDN Web Docs offer a dedicated section on WebGL, providing detailed documentation, tutorials, and interactive examples. It's an excellent resource for both beginners and advanced learners. You can explore WebGL concepts, create interactive graphics, and build your projects with the help of MDN's guides.

5. LearningWebGL.com

LearningWebGL.com offers a series of tutorials that guide you through the fundamentals of WebGL. Starting with basic concepts, it gradually introduces more advanced topics like shaders and textures. The tutorials include code examples and interactive demos, making it a great resource for hands-on learning.

6. WebGL Academy

WebGL Academy features tutorials and resources for WebGL developers. It covers various aspects of WebGL, including the basics, shaders, and advanced techniques like post-processing effects. The website provides clear explanations and code samples to help you grasp each topic.

7. YouTube Tutorials

YouTube hosts a wealth of video tutorials on WebGL. Many content creators offer step-by-step guides, coding demonstrations, and WebGL project walkthroughs. Exploring video tutorials can be an engaging way to learn WebGL, as you can follow along with practical examples.

8. Online Courses

Several online platforms, such as Coursera, edX, and Udemy, offer courses on WebGL and 3D graphics programming. These courses often include video lectures, assignments, and quizzes to reinforce your understanding. Consider enrolling in a structured course if you prefer a guided learning experience.

9. GitHub Repositories

GitHub hosts numerous repositories with WebGL projects, examples, and code snippets. Exploring these repositories can provide insights into real-world WebGL implementation. You can study the code, contribute to open-source projects, or create your WebGL projects on GitHub.

In summary, books and tutorials are valuable resources for mastering WebGL. Whether you prefer structured learning from books or interactive online tutorials, these recommendations cover a wide range of topics and skill levels. Combining multiple learning sources can help you gain a comprehensive understanding of WebGL and its applications in 3D web graphics development.

19.4. Attending Conferences and Workshops

Attending conferences and workshops is a fantastic way to enhance your knowledge, network with professionals, and stay updated with the latest trends in WebGL development. In this section, we'll explore the benefits of participating in these events and provide some tips on how to make the most of them.

Benefits of Conference and Workshop Attendance

1. **Learning from Experts**: Conferences and workshops often feature sessions and talks by industry experts and experienced developers. These presentations can provide valuable insights, practical tips, and in-depth knowledge about WebGL and related technologies.
2. **Networking Opportunities**: These events offer a unique chance to connect with like-minded individuals, potential collaborators, and professionals in the field. Networking can lead to new opportunities, collaborations, and friendships that can benefit your career.
3. **Staying Updated**: The web development and WebGL landscapes are constantly evolving. Conferences and workshops showcase the latest tools, techniques, and advancements, keeping you up-to-date with the current state of the industry.
4. **Hands-On Workshops**: Many events include hands-on workshops where you can practice your skills in a guided environment. These workshops can help you gain practical experience and improve your proficiency in WebGL.
5. **Inspiration and Creativity**: Exposure to a diverse range of

projects and ideas can inspire your creativity. You may discover innovative approaches, creative solutions, and fresh perspectives on web graphics and WebGL development.

Tips for Conference and Workshop Attendance

Here are some tips to maximize your experience when attending conferences and workshops related to WebGL:

1. **Plan Ahead**: Research the event's schedule and choose sessions, workshops, or talks that align with your interests and goals. Create a schedule to make the most of your time.
2. **Engage in Discussions**: Don't hesitate to ask questions during sessions or participate in panel discussions. Engaging with speakers and fellow attendees can lead to valuable insights and connections.
3. **Network Actively**: Attend networking sessions, social events, and after-parties. Strike up conversations with other attendees, share your experiences, and exchange contact information for future collaborations.
4. **Take Notes**: Bring a notebook or use a digital note-taking app to jot down key takeaways, ideas, and interesting concepts. These notes will serve as valuable references when you return to your work.
5. **Prepare Questions**: If you have specific questions or challenges related to WebGL, prepare them in advance. You can ask speakers, workshop instructors, or fellow attendees for advice and solutions.
6. **Collaborate and Share**: Be open to collaboration. Share your own experiences, projects, and knowledge with others. Collaboration often leads to new opportunities and

a deeper understanding of the subject matter.

7. **Stay Connected**: Follow up with the people you meet at the event. Connect with them on professional networks like LinkedIn or through email. Building and maintaining relationships can be a long-term asset.
8. **Evaluate and Reflect**: After the event, take time to reflect on what you've learned and how you can apply it to your projects. Consider how attending the event has impacted your skills and career goals.
9. **Consider Speaking**: If you gain expertise in WebGL, consider presenting at future conferences or workshops. Sharing your knowledge can solidify your understanding and contribute to the community.

Notable WebGL and Web Graphics Events

Here are some well-known conferences and workshops related to WebGL and web graphics:

- **SIGGRAPH**: SIGGRAPH is one of the most prestigious computer graphics conferences. It covers a wide range of topics, including WebGL and interactive 3D graphics.

- **WebGL Meetups**: Many cities have WebGL meetup groups that organize regular events, talks, and workshops. Check if there's a local meetup in your area.

- **WebGL Developers Conference**: This conference focuses exclusively on WebGL and offers sessions, workshops, and discussions on web graphics development.

- **Web3D Conference**: Web3D is an annual conference dedicated to 3D web technologies, including WebGL. It explores the integration of 3D graphics into web applications and platforms.

- **WebXR Dev Summit**: If you're interested in the intersection of WebGL and virtual or augmented reality, the WebXR Dev Summit is a relevant event.

In conclusion, attending conferences and workshops can be a pivotal part of your journey as a WebGL developer. It provides opportunities for learning, networking, and personal growth. By actively participating and staying engaged, you can make the most of these events and advance your skills and career in WebGL development.

19.5. Contributing to Open Source WebGL Projects

Contributing to open-source WebGL projects can be a fulfilling way to give back to the community, improve your skills, and collaborate with developers worldwide. In this section, we'll explore the benefits of contributing to open source and provide guidance on how to get started.

Benefits of Open Source Contribution

1. **Skill Enhancement**: Contributing to open-source projects allows you to work on real-world codebases, helping you become a better programmer and gain practical experience.
2. **Building a Portfolio**: Open source contributions are an excellent addition to your portfolio. They showcase your ability to collaborate, solve problems, and work with others

on a shared codebase.

3. **Community Engagement**: Engaging with open source communities exposes you to diverse perspectives, ideas, and best practices. You'll have the opportunity to learn from experienced developers.
4. **Giving Back**: By contributing to open source, you're contributing to the greater good of the developer community. Your work can benefit others and make a positive impact on the industry.
5. **Networking**: Collaborating with developers on open source projects can lead to valuable connections and potential job opportunities.

Getting Started with Open Source Contribution

Here's a step-by-step guide on how to get started with open source contribution in the context of WebGL:

1. **Choose a Project**: Select an open-source WebGL project that aligns with your interests and skills. It's essential to find a project that resonates with you.
2. **Study the Documentation**: Carefully read the project's documentation, including its README file and contribution guidelines. Understand the project's goals, coding standards, and workflow.
3. **Explore the Codebase**: Familiarize yourself with the project's codebase by browsing through the source code and documentation. Get a sense of its structure and architecture.
4. **Join the Community**: Most open-source projects have a community chat or forum where contributors discuss ideas and issues. Join these channels to introduce yourself and ask questions.

5. **Identify Issues**: Look for "good first issue" or "beginner-friendly" labels on the project's issue tracker. These are tasks that are suitable for newcomers.
6. **Fork the Repository**: Fork the project's repository on GitHub or the platform of your choice. This creates a copy of the project under your GitHub account.
7. **Set Up Your Development Environment**: Follow the project's guidelines to set up your development environment. This may involve installing dependencies and configuring tools.
8. **Work on an Issue**: Choose an issue to work on, and create a new branch for your changes. Make the necessary code changes, adhering to the project's coding standards.
9. **Write Tests**: If applicable, write tests for your code changes to ensure they don't introduce new issues.
10. **Submit a Pull Request**: Once you've made your changes and tested them, submit a pull request (PR) to the project's repository. Describe your changes and reference the related issue.
11. **Review and Iterate**: Be prepared for feedback from the project maintainers and community. Address any requested changes and iterate on your PR.
12. **Celebrate Your Contribution**: Once your PR is accepted and merged, celebrate your contribution to the open-source project. You've made a positive impact!

Tips for Successful Contribution

To make your open source contribution journey smoother, here are some tips:

- Start small: Begin with simple tasks to get accustomed to the project's workflow and coding style.

- Communicate openly: If you're unsure about something, don't hesitate to ask for help or clarification from the community.

- Be patient: Open source projects may have slower response times due to the volunteer nature of contributions. Be patient while waiting for feedback.

- Follow best practices: Adhere to coding standards, write clear and concise commit messages, and be respectful of others' contributions.

- Contribute regularly: Consistent contributions help you build a strong presence in the open source community and establish your expertise.

Notable WebGL Open Source Projects

Here are a few open-source WebGL projects and libraries you can consider contributing to:

- **Three.js**: A popular JavaScript 3D library that simplifies WebGL development.

- **Babylon.js**: A powerful and feature-rich open-source framework for building 3D games and simulations.

- **Regl**: A fast functional WebGL framework suitable for creating highly performant web graphics.

- **GLSL Sandbox**: An open platform for sharing WebGL shaders, where you can contribute your own shaders and experiments.

- **PlayCanvas Engine**: An open-source WebGL game engine for building interactive 3D content.

In conclusion, contributing to open-source WebGL projects can be a rewarding experience that benefits both you and the broader developer community. It's an opportunity to learn, grow, and make a positive impact while collaborating with like-minded individuals worldwide.

Chapter 20: The Future of WebGL and Beyond

20.1. Predicting the Evolution of WebGL

As we look ahead to the future of WebGL, it's essential to consider the trends and possibilities that may shape this technology. While we can't predict the future with certainty, we can identify some key areas where WebGL is likely to evolve:

1. Performance Improvements

WebGL performance has been steadily improving over the years, thanks to advancements in web browsers, graphics hardware, and the WebGL specification itself. Expect even more performance gains as technology continues to evolve. This will enable more complex and immersive 3D experiences on the web.

2. Integration with Emerging Web Technologies

WebGL is likely to integrate more closely with other emerging web technologies. This includes WebAssembly (Wasm), which allows running low-level code in web browsers, and WebGPU, a new standard for high-performance graphics and computation on the web. These integrations will expand the capabilities of WebGL and open up new possibilities.

3. WebXR Integration

WebXR, an API for building virtual and augmented reality experiences on the web, will continue to grow in importance. WebGL will play a crucial role in rendering 3D content for WebXR experiences, making it an essential component of the immersive web.

4. Accessibility and Inclusivity

As the web strives to become more accessible and inclusive, WebGL developers will need to consider accessibility features and guidelines. This includes ensuring that 3D content is usable by individuals with disabilities, such as providing alternative text for 3D objects.

5. Cross-Platform Compatibility

Cross-platform compatibility will remain a priority. WebGL content should work seamlessly across different devices, browsers, and operating systems. This ensures that users have a consistent experience, regardless of their choice of technology.

6. Education and Training

WebGL will continue to be a valuable tool for education and training. It enables interactive 3D simulations and visualizations for a wide range of educational purposes, from science and engineering to art and history.

7. Real-time Collaboration

Collaborative 3D applications will become more prevalent. WebGL-powered platforms will allow users to collaborate in real time on 3D models, designs, and virtual environments. This has implications for industries such as architecture, engineering, and game development.

8. Sustainability and Efficiency

Efforts to make web content more sustainable and energy-efficient will extend to WebGL. Developers will seek ways to optimize 3D graphics rendering to reduce energy consumption and minimize the environmental impact of web-based 3D experiences.

9. Enhanced Development Tools

Expect improvements in WebGL development tools and frameworks. Streamlined workflows, debugging tools, and libraries will make it easier for developers to create high-quality 3D web content.

10. Ethical Considerations

As WebGL becomes more prominent, ethical considerations will come to the forefront. Developers will need to consider the responsible use of 3D technology, addressing issues such as privacy, security, and the impact of 3D content on society.

In summary, the future of WebGL holds exciting possibilities for developers and users alike. With continued advancements in performance, integration with emerging technologies, and a focus on accessibility and inclusivity, WebGL is set to play a significant role in the evolving web ecosystem. Developers should stay informed about these trends and actively participate in shaping the future of WebGL through contributions, experimentation, and responsible development practices.

20.2. The Convergence of WebGL and Emerging Technologies

WebGL is on a path of convergence with various emerging technologies, creating exciting opportunities for web developers and users. This convergence enables the integration of WebGL with cutting-edge trends, expanding the possibilities for web-based graphics and interactive experiences. Here are some key areas where WebGL is converging with other technologies:

1. WebXR and Immersive Experiences

One of the most significant convergences is with WebXR, which includes both WebVR (Virtual Reality) and WebAR (Augmented Reality). These APIs allow developers to create immersive 3D experiences that can be accessed through web browsers. WebGL plays a pivotal role in rendering 3D content for WebXR, making it a core component of the immersive web.

2. WebAssembly (Wasm)

WebGL and WebAssembly are a natural pairing. Wasm allows developers to run low-level code in web browsers at near-native speeds. When combined with WebGL, it enables high-performance graphics and computation within web applications. This convergence enhances the capabilities of web-based 3D graphics and simulations.

3. WebGPU

WebGPU is a modern web standard for low-level graphics and computation, designed to replace WebGL in the long run. While WebGL remains widely supported, WebGPU offers better performance and improved GPU access. Over time, we can expect a transition from WebGL to WebGPU for more demanding 3D applications.

4. 3D Printing and WebGL

WebGL's convergence with 3D printing technologies opens up possibilities for online 3D modeling and customization. Users can interact with 3D models in real time, making adjustments and optimizations before sending the final design to a 3D printer. WebGL-powered web applications can facilitate this process.

5. Machine Learning and AI Integration

Machine learning and AI technologies are increasingly integrated into web applications. WebGL's ability to handle complex visual data makes it valuable for visualizing machine learning models and AI-generated content. This convergence supports the creation of AI-driven interactive experiences on the web.

6. Blockchain and NFTs

The world of blockchain and non-fungible tokens (NFTs) has seen a surge in interest. WebGL can be used to create interactive and visually stunning NFT showcases, enabling artists and creators to present their digital assets in unique ways. This convergence bridges the gap between blockchain and the interactive web.

7. Web3 and Decentralized Applications

WebGL has a role to play in the development of decentralized applications (DApps) in the Web3 ecosystem. These DApps often require 3D visualizations and simulations, and WebGL can provide the necessary rendering capabilities for creating engaging and immersive decentralized experiences.

8. Accessibility and Inclusivity

As WebGL converges with these technologies, it's crucial to prioritize accessibility and inclusivity. Developers must ensure that immersive experiences created with WebGL are usable by individuals with disabilities. This includes providing alternative text and user-friendly controls for 3D content.

In conclusion, the convergence of WebGL with emerging technologies is transforming the web into a platform for sophisticated 3D graphics, immersive experiences, and innovative applications. This convergence creates opportunities for developers to push the boundaries of what's possible on the web and deliver engaging, interactive content to users across various devices and platforms. As these technologies continue to evolve, WebGL remains at the forefront of web-based 3D graphics, enabling the creation of the next generation of web experiences.

20.3. WebGL and WebAssembly (Wasm)

WebGL and WebAssembly (Wasm) are two powerful technologies that have been on a convergence path, opening up new possibilities for web developers and users alike. This section explores the relationship between WebGL and WebAssembly, highlighting their strengths and the advantages of combining them in web applications.

1. High-Performance Computing

WebAssembly is designed for high-performance computing in web browsers. It allows developers to run code at near-native speeds, making it an ideal choice for computationally intensive tasks. When WebGL and WebAssembly are used together, developers can harness the power of the GPU (Graphics Processing Unit) for tasks such as physics simulations, data visualization, and image processing, achieving remarkable performance gains.

2. Portability

One of the key benefits of WebAssembly is its portability. WebAssembly modules are compiled to a binary format that can be executed on any platform that supports WebAssembly, including browsers across different operating systems. This means that WebGL applications utilizing WebAssembly can run consistently and efficiently on a wide range of devices, ensuring a seamless user experience.

3. Memory Efficiency

WebGL applications often deal with large datasets and complex 3D models. WebAssembly's memory management capabilities allow for efficient handling of these data structures, reducing memory consumption and improving overall application stability. This is particularly important for web applications that require real-time rendering and interactivity.

4. Cross-Browser Compatibility

WebAssembly enjoys broad support across modern web browsers, ensuring cross-browser compatibility for WebGL applications that rely on WebAssembly. This eliminates the need for browser-specific workarounds and enables developers to target a wider audience with their WebGL-powered projects.

5. Interoperability

WebAssembly can interface seamlessly with JavaScript, which is the primary language for WebGL development. This means that developers can easily integrate WebAssembly modules into their existing WebGL applications. This interoperability allows for the reuse of existing JavaScript code and the incorporation of WebAssembly for performance-critical sections.

6. Security

WebAssembly runs in a sandboxed environment, providing an additional layer of security for web applications. This sandboxing ensures that WebAssembly code cannot access sensitive user data or perform malicious actions. When integrated with WebGL, this security feature is valuable for protecting users' privacy and data.

7. Optimizing WebGL Applications

Developers can optimize WebGL applications by offloading certain computational tasks to WebAssembly modules. For example, complex physics simulations or data processing can be handled more efficiently in WebAssembly, leaving the GPU to focus on rendering. This approach can lead to smoother and more responsive WebGL applications.

8. Future Potential

As both WebGL and WebAssembly continue to evolve, their convergence is expected to lead to even more advanced web applications. This includes the development of sophisticated games, simulations, data visualizations, and interactive experiences that were previously challenging to achieve on the web. The combination of these technologies holds great promise for the future of web-based graphics and applications.

In summary, the convergence of WebGL and WebAssembly brings together the strengths of high-performance graphics rendering and efficient, portable code execution. This combination empowers developers to create immersive and responsive web applications that can run seamlessly across various platforms and browsers. It also positions WebGL at the forefront of modern web development, enabling the creation of visually stunning and interactive experiences for users worldwide.

20.4. Future Challenges and Opportunities

The field of WebGL and web-based 3D graphics is dynamic and continually evolving. As we look to the future, there are several challenges and opportunities that developers, businesses, and the broader web community should consider.

1. Performance Optimization

While WebGL has made significant strides in performance optimization, there is always room for improvement. As web applications become more complex and demanding, developers will need to find innovative ways to further optimize rendering pipelines, reduce load times, and enhance overall performance. This includes leveraging new rendering techniques, optimizing shader code, and implementing efficient culling algorithms.

2. Standardization and Interoperability

The WebGL ecosystem would benefit from greater standardization and interoperability. Ensuring that WebGL implementations across different browsers and devices are consistent can simplify development and testing processes. Additionally, improved interoperability with other web technologies, such as WebXR for virtual and augmented reality, can open up new possibilities for immersive web experiences.

3. Accessibility and Inclusivity

Accessibility remains a crucial consideration for WebGL and 3D web content. Ensuring that 3D graphics are accessible to users with disabilities is essential. Developers should focus on providing alternative text descriptions, keyboard navigation, and other accessibility features to make WebGL applications more inclusive.

4. WebAssembly Integration

As mentioned earlier, the integration of WebAssembly with WebGL is a promising avenue for performance optimization. Exploring how WebAssembly can be used to accelerate various aspects of WebGL applications, from physics simulations to AI-driven experiences, presents exciting opportunities for developers.

5. Cross-Platform Compatibility

With the proliferation of devices and platforms, ensuring cross-platform compatibility for WebGL applications is a challenge. Developers must consider varying screen sizes, input methods, and performance capabilities when creating 3D web content. Implementing responsive design principles and utilizing frameworks that support multiple platforms can help address this challenge.

6. Security

As WebGL applications become more sophisticated, security remains a top concern. Developers must stay vigilant in protecting user data and privacy. This includes implementing secure communication protocols, preventing unauthorized access to WebGL content, and regularly updating security measures.

7. Education and Training

There is a growing demand for skilled WebGL developers. Educational institutions and online learning platforms should continue to offer courses and resources to train the next generation of 3D web developers. Providing accessible learning materials can help bridge the skills gap in this field.

8. Content Creation Tools

Improvements in 3D modeling and content creation tools are essential for the growth of WebGL. Developers and artists need user-friendly software that simplifies the process of creating 3D assets for the web. The availability of such tools can democratize 3D content creation and make it more accessible to a broader audience.

9. Collaboration and Community

The WebGL community plays a vital role in advancing the technology. Collaboration between developers, artists, educators, and researchers can drive innovation and foster the sharing of best practices. Participation in forums, conferences, and open-source projects can help strengthen the WebGL ecosystem.

10. Ethical Considerations

WebGL applications have the potential to influence and shape user experiences. Developers and businesses should consider the ethical implications of their creations, including issues related to user consent, data privacy, and the impact on society. Responsible development practices and ethical considerations are essential for the long-term success of WebGL.

In conclusion, WebGL and web-based 3D graphics offer exciting opportunities for creativity, innovation, and immersive user experiences. However, addressing the challenges mentioned above and embracing the opportunities they present will be key to the continued growth and success of WebGL in the ever-evolving landscape of web development. By working together and staying informed about emerging trends and technologies, the WebGL community can shape the future of 3D graphics on the web.

20.5. Preparing for the Next Wave in Web Graphics

As we look ahead to the future of web graphics beyond WebGL, it's evident that the landscape of web development is in a constant state of evolution. Here, we'll explore some trends and considerations that can help developers and businesses prepare for the next wave in web graphics.

1. WebGL and WebAssembly Integration

WebAssembly (Wasm) has gained significant traction as a technology that can enhance the performance of web applications. The integration of WebGL with WebAssembly can lead to even more powerful and efficient web graphics experiences. Developers should keep an eye on advancements in this area, as it could unlock new possibilities for graphics-intensive applications.

2. WebGPU and Low-Level Graphics APIs

WebGPU is an emerging web standard that provides low-level access to GPU (Graphics Processing Unit) capabilities. It aims to offer improved performance and greater control over graphics rendering. As WebGPU becomes more widely adopted, developers may have the opportunity to leverage this technology for high-performance web graphics.

3. Real-time Ray Tracing

Real-time ray tracing is a rendering technique that simulates the behavior of light rays in a scene, resulting in highly realistic graphics. While traditionally used in offline rendering, advancements in hardware and software are making real-time ray tracing feasible on the web. This technology can significantly enhance the visual quality of web graphics.

4. Machine Learning and AI

Machine learning and artificial intelligence (AI) are increasingly being integrated into web graphics applications. From enhancing image quality to enabling interactive experiences driven by AI, developers can explore ways to leverage machine learning models and techniques to create more intelligent and dynamic web graphics.

5. Web 3.0 and Decentralized Graphics

Web 3.0, often associated with blockchain and decentralized technologies, introduces new possibilities for web graphics. Decentralized platforms can empower artists and creators to distribute and monetize their 3D content directly on the web, bypassing traditional intermediaries.

6. Accessibility and Inclusivity

As web graphics continue to advance, it's crucial to prioritize accessibility and inclusivity. Ensuring that all users, including those with disabilities, can interact with and enjoy web graphics is a responsibility that developers should uphold. This includes providing alternative text, keyboard navigation, and other accessibility features.

7. Environmental Considerations

With the increasing complexity and demand for web graphics, developers should also consider the environmental impact. Optimizing graphics rendering to reduce energy consumption and carbon emissions is a growing concern. Efficient algorithms and rendering techniques can contribute to more eco-friendly web graphics.

8. Collaboration and Standards

Collaboration within the web development community and adherence to web standards will continue to be essential. Developers should actively participate in discussions, contribute to open-source projects, and advocate for best practices in web graphics.

9. Education and Training

The demand for skilled web graphics developers is expected to grow. Education and training programs should adapt to cover emerging technologies and trends in web graphics. Online courses, workshops, and certification programs can help individuals acquire the necessary skills.

10. Ethical and Privacy Considerations

As web graphics become more immersive and data-intensive, ethical and privacy considerations become increasingly important. Developers and businesses should prioritize user data protection, informed consent, and responsible data handling practices.

In conclusion, the future of web graphics holds exciting opportunities and challenges. Staying informed about emerging technologies, fostering collaboration, and maintaining a commitment to accessibility and ethics will be crucial for developers and businesses looking to thrive in the ever-evolving world of web graphics. By embracing these trends and considerations, we can collectively shape a more innovative, inclusive, and sustainable future for web graphics on the internet.

www.ingramcontent.com/pod-product-compliance
Lightning Source LLC
LaVergne TN
LVHW090304210926
848480LV00001B/123
* 9 7 9 8 2 2 4 2 7 3 3 8 6 *